They Were Giants 2008

They Were Giants 2008

Patrick Yearly

iUniverse, Inc.
New York Lincoln Shanghai

They Were Giants 2008

iUniverse books may be ordered through booksellers or by contacting:

iUniverse
2021 Pine Lake Road, Suite 100
Lincoln, NE 68512
www.iuniverse.com
1-800-Authors (1-800-288-4677)

Because of the dynamic nature of the Internet, any Web addresses or links contained in this book may have changed since publication and may no longer be valid.

The views expressed in this work are solely those of the author and do not necessarily reflect the views of the publisher, and the publisher hereby disclaims any responsibility for them.

ISBN: 978-0-595-48945-9 (pbk)
ISBN: 978-0-595-60903-1 (ebk)

Printed in the United States of America

Contents

Introduction

Each day we walk outside our front door into a stimulating world. The opportunity to live a long and fulfilling life has never been greater. In quiet solitude, many men and women spend their lives creating small stepping-stones that lead to a greater good. Their work goes unnoticed to society, but their impact is enormous. We don't see them on television or read about them in the newspaper. They don't appear on the covers of magazines or on the silver screen. We never see them holding a press conference or taking center stage. They come from every arena in life: science, technology, business, medicine, the arts. The list is endless. They go about their work with a dedication that does not attract attention and constant gratification. Their reward is in knowing that they have made a difference.

This book contains snapshots of these anonymous people whose deaths were reported in the media between October 1, 2006 to October 1, 2007. It was not my intention to write a book of obituaries, but a collection of the achievements of a group of people whose work has benefited many. Writing an extended story about each person would result in an unmanageable book of more than a thousand pages. Actually, in most cases there is only a limited amount of information available. I hope that these stories can be used as a source of reference so you can take a few minutes to reflect on how a small group of people could affect so many lives with so little attention given to their contributions.

This, however, is not an obscure group whose passing went unnoticed. Their work received a salute from prominent newspapers, magazines, websites and television stations throughout the world, but they were not the lead story and no one was mourning their loss around the water cooler at the office the next day. Some were well known within the inner circle of their field, but none was a household name. A few may have been well recognized decades ago, but no longer.

I have categorized their efforts into ten categories. Some sections may be easier to read and appeal more to you than others and some stories are more colorful than others. The science category, for example, can be a bit tedious to read, but that should not diminish what they did. Also, people do not die in a logical fashion. There are categories that highlight many more people than in other sections. Perhaps the numbers may be quite different next year. The selection of people whose stories are represented in this book are mine alone and certainly subject to debate. I am not promoting any point of view in support of any cause.

This book is the fourth in a series of annual installments. Nearly 300 people are represented in the 2008 edition. Ultimately, in the end the focus is not on them, but on a world that benefits immeasurably from their work. Without their resolve we would all be much poorer.

ARTS

Fancy Pants

The business began by importing and reproducing French designs with an emphasis on the collections of Dior and Balenciaga. After casually making evening wear for herself and her prominent friends, including Jackie Kennedy, Elizabeth Taylor and Audrey Hepburn, **Irene Galizine**'s first fashion show in 1959 was quite a success. Her collections were praised as the highlight of the season. Most recognized was the design of evening pants she introduced that had either slim and embroidered features or accented gaudy fabrics and were called "palazzo pajamas". It was Irene's presentation of her designs at great society parties that inspired women to buy her creations. The most famous palazzo pajamas were worn by Claudia Cardinale in the original Pink Panther movie and have continued to be exhibited in many fashion retrospectives. Irene was known as 'Princess Irene' Galizine as she was a descendant of Russian nobility.

Jaws

Stuck in traffic on the Los Angeles freeway during a rainstorm, tuba player **Tommy Johnson** was late to the first recording session for director Steven Spielberg's now classic movie Jaws. He noticed that he had to continually play a big, long tuba solo that had been created for the film score by the legendary John Williams. The thick, heavy "bom, bom, bom, bom" sound heard with each approach of the shark in the movie became recognizable throughout the United States and an instant hit. In addition to his work in Jaws, Tommy played tuba on thousands of film scores over nearly 50 years. Among the list of films he worked on: "The Godfather", "Close Encounters of the Third Kind", "Indiana Jones", "The Lion King", "Titanic" and "Star Trek".

Glassmaker

The work seemed to contain items of **Timo Sarpaneva**'s native Finland. Critics said he showed light as if seen from beneath the ice that covers the sea or in the leaves of a forest. He called his glass magical because of its constant changes and expressiveness. Timo was described as the last of a generation of Finns who helped to make Scandanavia's clean, simple line a modern standard. His works found their way into art museums, stylish dining rooms and textbooks on design. In the 1960's he developed a method of blowing glass into a charred wooden mold to create a surface that resembled cracked ice. Many of his most popular drinkware designs imitate the icy beverages they hold. His many awards included three grand prizes at the Milan Triennale, which has been called the Olympics of the design world.

Creative Travel Writer

The first excursion was at age 18 as an apprentice aboard a four-masted Finnish grain ship bound for Australia. Next came a voyage by station wagon, foot and horseback to climb Mir Samir, a 20,000-foot peak in a wild region of Afghanistan despite never having climbed a mountain. He never did make it to the top and, at just a few thousand feet from the summit, stopped to read a pamphlet on how to climb mountains. **Eric Newby** was considered the dean of postwar British travel writing as he spent more than 50 years visiting some of the world's most remote places. Among his other adventures, Eric and his wife traveled down the Ganges River in an enormous boat that ran aground after 200 yards and required 32 men to carry it overland. One winter found them uncomfortably touring a damp Ireland by bicycle.

The Queen of Musical Parody

Dreams of being an opera diva did not work out so **Anna Russell** did the next best thing—she made fun of them for a living. She jokingly claimed that her career began as the "leading soprano of the Ellis Island Opera Company" and said that she learned to play the French horn from a research article. Her most renowned spoofs came from the operas of Wagner and Gilbert and Sullivan. In 1952 she performed in 37 cities in the United States and Canada before 100,000 listeners. He record, "Ann Russell Sings?" became a best seller. She made fun of bad voices and bad teaching with her success coming at the height of popularity for classical music. Her goal of becoming an opera singer was ruined at sixteen when she was struck by a hockey stick and her acoustical voice was damaged. Although she no longer had range, Anna said that, as a result of the injury, she was able to sing louder and louder and more awful.

Contemporary Art Director

Museums should be user-friendly meeting places that challenge accepted ideas and embrace a wide range of artists and time periods. So thought **Pontus Hulten** whose achievements in art spanned many countries and the founding directorships of several museums, including the celebrated Pompidou Center in Paris and the Museum of Contemporary Art in Los Angeles. He was among the first of postwar Europe's curator impresarios. His exhibitions were considered extraordinary in scope, including the opportunity to show Picasso's traveling show of the famed "Guernica" painting for the National Museum of Sweden in the 1950's. Pontus was often credited with inventing the interdisciplinary exhibit and the idea of organizing shows working with other teams of curators.

Elvis of the Rio Grande

It took 25 years before **Freddy Fender** was able to top the charts. Starting as a balladeer in the 1950's, he performed rock covers in Spanish as 'El Be-Bop Kid'. By 1975 he had topped the pop charts in English with "Before the Next Teardrop Falls". In the early 1990's he teamed with three other elder statesmen of the Tex-Mex sound to form the Texas Tornados and spread Tex-Mex music to a wider audience. Freddy joked to People magazine "you've heard of New Kids on the Block? Well, we're the old farts in the neighborhood". In all, he won a Grammy outright and shared two others.

A Hollywood Original

He was capable of a dud or a masterpiece due to his riverboat gambler style of film directing. **Robert Altman** was considered to be the last of a breed. He was praised for his improvisational style and groundbreaking use of multiplayer soundtracks. In all, he received five Academy Award nominations for Best Director—"MASH, "Nashville", "The Player", "Short Cuts" and "Gosford Park". He never won and his only Oscar was an honorary award received in 2006. One critic called "MASH" the best American war comedy since sound arrived. In his early years, in the 1950's, Robert got his feet wet with directing assignments for such classic TV shows as "Alfred Hitchcock Presents", "Maverick", "Peter Gunn", "Bonanza", "Hawaiian Eye", "Route 66" and "Combat".

Science Fiction Writer

For nearly 80 years **Jack Williamson** churned out science fiction stories that included more than 50 novels. His first short story, "The Metal Man", was published in 1928, the year after Charles Lindbergh had made the first solo plane flight across the Atlantic. He was a pioneer of the genre and one of the longest active writers in the field. His work focused on robotics, genetic engineering and the colonization of the planets. Jack believed that science was the door to the future and science fiction was the golden key. His awards were numerous: a Grandmaster Award for lifetime achievement from the Science Fiction Writers of America, a World Fantasy Award and the Bram Stoker Award from the Horror Writers Association. He was a mentor to many writers, including the legendary science fiction writer Ray Bradbury.

Desegregating the Metropolitan Opera

At first he performed with the New York City Opera, the National Negro Opera Company and the New England Opera Company. By 1953 **Robert McFerrin Sr.** had won the Metropolitan Opera's "Auditions of the Air" radio contest, but listeners didn't know he was an African-American. Two years later the baritone became the first black man to sing on stage at the Met performing in Aida. The celebrated Marian Anderson had become the first black woman to perform there just three weeks earlier. At the end of the decade Robert made it to Hollywood when he dubbed Sidney Poitier's voice in the film version of "Porgy and Bess". He toured extensively while showcasing his talent in Negro spirituals and German art songs.

Documentarian of Nigerian Culture

After a start as a medical photographer, **Frank Speed** found his calling as an ethnographic filmmaker in Nigeria. Some of his many projects recording the arts and cultures of Nigeria have become classics that are still widely used in African studies and anthropology courses around the world. Beginning in the 1950's, Frank made nine films on medical subjects, including one which recorded the world's last major smallpox epidemic. Later, he moved into work that filmed arts and ceremonies that were dying out and celebrated the vitality of the cultures that had produced them.

Geometric Painter

Never motivated by money, **Roy Newell** remained outside the art world mainstream and produced fewer than 100 paintings. His talent lie as a vivid colorist who dedicated himself to creating irregular pattern paintings that resembled quilted fields of color. As one of the original members of the American Abstract Expressionists, Roy would often rework his paintings over decades and slowly build up the geometric shapes and surfaces in countless layers by using great densities of paint. Some paintings are an inch thick. He had much difficulty in parting with his work and rarely had public showings in a career of nearly 70 years.

Pioneering R & B Singer

Known as "Miss Rhythm", **Ruth Brown** was among the elite black pop singers of the early 1950's. Many of her recordings topped the R & B charts, including her most recognized tunes "Teardrops From My Eyes" and "(Mama) He Treats Your Daughter Mean". Little Richard made it known that he took his well recognized squeal from Ruth. A member of the Rock and Roll Hall of Fame, she won both a Grammy and a Tony award. When popular tastes changed, Ruth went to work for a period of time as a maid. In the late 1980's, she helped to create the Rhythm and Blues Foundation in Philadelphia to recover her back royalties as well as those of nearly three dozen other performers.

Outsider Art

He first got noticed when he hung his paintings on trees. Self-taught, **Mose Tolliver** began painting after he was severely injured in a factory accident. His self-portraits and vivid images of nature, people, animals and the female form were done with house paint. Called "Outsider Art", Mose' work was influenced by what he drew from his life in a simple and direct style. Among the museums that now display his work are: the American Folk Art Museum in New York, the High Museum of Art in Atlanta, the Milwaukee Art Museum, the Smithsonian, the New Orleans Museum of Art and the American Visionary Art Museum in Baltimore.

The Hits of Broadway

For more than 60 years **Betty Comden** teamed with Adolph Green to form one of Broadway's most celebrated songwriting duos. In addition, they penned many classics for the silver screen. Such stage shows as "On the Town", "Wonderful Town", "Peter Pan" and "Bells are Ringing" benefited from their talents as well as the film musicals "Singin in the Rain" and "The Band Wagon". Working with such legendary composers as Leonard Bernstein, Jule Styne and Andre Previn, they created the anthem-like New York, New York" as well as "The Party's Over", "It's Love" and "Some Other 'Time". They won numerous Tony Awards and were among the recipients of the 1991 Kennedy Center honors for their contributions to American musical theater.

Early Folk Ballads

Sex, betrayal and all manner of murder. It sounds like the basis for a contemporary novel, but **Albert Friedman** revived the centerpiece of behavior captured in the preliterate Middle Age popular ballads. A book he published in 1956, "The Viking Book of Folk Ballads of the English-Speaking World" helped to renew interest in traditional English and Scottish ballads that reached its high point in the late 1950's and early 60's. It contained a compilation of traditional songs from Britain and America that recorded a wide range of experience, including romantic tragedies, supernatural events and the exploits of cowboys and outlaws. Albert said that ballads are songs or performances and not poems. Many of the songs he included in the book became the basis for songs by Joan Baez and Bob Dylan.

Painter of Marine Life

Wandering the world for more than 40 years, **Stanley Meltzoff** would spend his days peering at fish and then diving to great depths of more than 100 feet to photograph them. Once back in his studio, he transformed those images into vibrant paintings for magazines such as Sports Illustrated and Scientific American. It was an understatement to say that water was in Stanley's blood. From Long Island to Key West to the Pacific atolls and the Mediterranean coast, he interacted with a wide variety of fish, and their many colors, in their natural environment that enabled him to recreate them vividly on canvas.

Photographer of the Impossible

Whenever there was a challenge **Yale Joel** was ready for it. He was a great practitioner of experimental photography with his 3-D and infrared work. His extraordinary measures to get the right shot earned him the nickname "photographer of the impossible". As an original staff member of Life Magazine, Yale relished assignments that required the use of special arcane equipment, carefully orchestrated setups and special effects. Among his most acclaimed photos: a group portrait of 1500 Disney World employees, a view of the Rockettes chorus line in perfect formation and a full image of the Time-Life building in Chicago taken just after its completion. The Time-Life shot was used with an 80 year-old wooden view camera with a bubble shaped extra-wide lens.

The Dawn of Reggae

"The Harder They Come" was a movie cult classic on American college campuses with one theater showing it for six years. The film was the first Jamaican originated feature and was produced, directed and co-written by **Perry Henzell**. The movie introduced a number of reggae songs, music that was unfamiliar outside of Jamaica. When it premiered in Kingston, Jamaica in 1972, 40,000 people showed up outside a theater that sat 1,500. The soundtrack album spread the gospel of reggae across the United States and paved the way for the acceptance of reggae legend Bob Marley.

The Jezebel of Jazz

It's difficult enough to succeed in one musical style, but **Anita O'Day** made her mark as both a big band and jazz singer. Starting out with the well-known swing band of Gene Krupa in 1941, she sang one of their greatest hits "Let Me Off Uptown". She moved on to the other well-recognized bands of Woody Herman and Stan Kenton and gave Kenton a hit with her rendition of "And Her Tears Flowed Like Wine". By 1945 she was named by Down Beat magazine as the Top Girl Band Vocalist and was voted by critics as the Outstanding New Star in Esquire magazine. Anita set her own path when she was on stage. In an era when most female singers made a glamorous presentation, she dressed up in the standard issue band jacket and skirt, giving herself a tomboy image. As the popularity of the big band sound faded in the 1950's, she made a name in jazz circles. It was said that she was the only white woman that belonged in the same breath as Ella Fitzgerald, Billie Holiday and Sarah Vaughan.

Tropicalia

A musical style that celebrates the combinations and contradictions of modern Brazilian culture with its collision of the old and the future, the elegant and the vulgar, Tropicalia found its greatest record producer in **Rogerio Duprat**. He was often compared to George Martin, the legendary producer of the Beatles. Rogerio would create songs with both brilliant and bizarre arrangements that were partially inspired by the Beatles, such as the imaginary clutter in "Strawberry Fields Forever". You could hear the elegant hush of bossa nova bump up against blaring carnival brass bands, the ritual religious drums of Afro-Brazilian music against swanky string arrangements after the style of a Sinatra record, crowd noises, sirens, the rhythm of the cha-cha-cha. Rogerio helped to crystallize the musical aspect of the multimedia connection that Tropicalia radiated.

X-Men

By the 1970's the original characters of the X-Men comic series had become worn out. First created in 1963, the series had never drawn significant fan interest. A team of fictitious mutants, the X-Men were formed as the result of an evolutionary glitch and born with latent superhuman abilities. With his talents as an illustrator, **Dave Cockrum** resurrected the series into what would become the most popular comic book series in America and a billion dollar movie empire. Thunderbird, Colossus, Nightcrawler and Storm became the heroes of a dozen comic book titles, cartoons and video games.

Carnival Songs

Braguinha had become an influential figure in Brazilian culture by adapting North American cartoons and children's songs to the tastes of Brazil. He would change a tale such as "The Three Little Pigs" and convert it into Portuguese, the country's native language. It wasn't unusual for him to take significant liberties with the translation and lyrics during an adaptation. Braguinha's songs were often celebrations of female sensuality and evocative of the lush tropics of Brazil. His most recognized song "Bullfights in Madrid" became a national obsession when fans chanted its verses during the 1950 World Cup in Rio de Janeiro when Brazil defeated Spain. The influence of his work extended to the Bossa Nova and Tropicalista music movements of the '50's and '60's. A seven foot bronze statue of Braguinha can be found in the famed Copacabana beach district in Rio.

Tommy

Although credited by critics with raising the Grands Ballet of Canada to international status and honored by the Canadian and Quebec governments for his contributions to Canadian dance, **Fernand Nault** spent many years as a dancer, teacher, choreographer and artistic director in the United States. His choreography of the rock opera "Tommy" by the Who became a hit ballet in 1970 and was performed over 300 times, drawing new dance audiences previously unfamiliar with ballet. Among the distinguished awards Fernand would later receive were the Order of Canada and the Prix Denise Pelletier, a lifetime achievement honor from the Quebec government.

The Green Lantern

He helped to preside over the golden age of comic books. It was a subway ride in Manhattan that inspired **Martin Nodell** in 1940. Seeing a trainman waving a lantern with a green light along the dark tracks inspired Martin to imagine a young engineer who would survive a train crash and discover an ancient lantern that had been created from a green meteor. His character, Alan Scott, builds a ring from the lamp that gives him superpowers to become a crime fighter. The first Green Lantern appearance was in July 1940 as an eight-page story. Martin would get his own series and he drew the character until 1947 using the name Matt Dellon. As if one classic creation wasn't enough, Martin was on the design team in the 1960's that helped to develop the Pillsbury Doughboy.

Quilt Artist

Critics compared her work to modernist paintings, jazz music and African textiles. The quilts of Rosie Lee Tompkins hung in museums and graced the pages of art magazines. Her insistence on remaining anonymous later on revealed that Rosie's real name was **Effie Mae Howard**. She enjoyed having her quilts exhibited as long as she didn't have to make a public appearance and use her real name. Her quilts were improvisational and marked by bold, lush colors, irregular edges and corners that don't meet at strict angles. After gaining attention in the 1980's Effie Mae's quilts were regularly featured in magazines and exhibited at university galleries and museums throughout the United States, including the High Museum of Art in Atlanta and the Whitney Museum of American Art in New York City.

The Concerned Photographer

In the wake of the Second World War, photojournalism became increasingly involved with human rights and civil rights. After photographing a black American soldier at the Berlin Wall in the early 1960's, **Leonard Freed** was struck by the contrast between his defense of liberty in the West and the civil rights movement at home. He followed the years of struggle against segregation and discrimination by the NAACP, photographing Martin Luther King, Jr. and his great march in the search for equality. Leonard's images of children playing around a fire hydrant in New York City captured the stark contrast in distinction between the races in 1960's America. With Life magazine publishing his work, Leonard made a great impact on readers across the nation. His 1968 book "Black in White America" covered race relations in both the North and South.

Music Industry Titan

He fell in love with music at the age of 9 when he went to see Duke Ellington and Cab Calloway at the Palladium Theater in London. Along with a partner, **Ahmet Ertegun** founded Atlantic Records in 1947 with an initial investment that he had borrowed from the family dentist. He was an astute judge of musical talent and business potential and surrounded himself with skillful people. Atlantic grew from a small independent label into a major national music company that helped to shape the careers of The Rolling Stones, Ray Charles, Led Zeppelin, Aretha Franklin, Otis Redding and John Coltrane. In 1957 Atlantic was among the first to record in stereo. He was a prime mover in starting the Rock and Roll Hall of Fame and Museum and was inducted into the hall in 1987. In addition to music, Ahmet and his brother co-founded the New York Cosmos of the North American Soccer League and brought in the legendary Pele to jump-start the team and league. Ahmet was also inducted into the National Soccer Hall of Fame in 2003.

Ground Breaking Woman Photographer

In a photographic style marked by dramatic lighting, pared-down compositions and materials from everyday life, **Ruth Bernhard** became known for her still-life photographs as well as her abstract images of female nudes. In the 1940's she became part of Group f/64, which included the celebrated photographers Ansel Adams and Dorothea Lange. Ruth took pictures almost exclusively in the studio and was known to take a single picture from one specific angle after setting up meticulously, sometimes over days. Her work is on display the San Francisco Museum of Modern Art, the Metropolitan Museum of Art in New York, the Museum of Fine Arts in Houston and the Victoria and Albert Museum in London.

Comedy TV Writer

It was one the most popular animated television series of the 1960's. "The Bullwinkle Show" featured Rocky the flying squirrel and the illustrious Bullwinkle J. Moose. Along for the ride was the dastardly Boris Badenov and Natasha Fatale who were featured in cold war spoofs on the show. **Chris Hayward** helped to write this segment of the show, but was most closely associated with "The Adventures of Dudley Do-Right" which followed the hapless royal Canadian Mountie in his never-ending pursuit of the evil Snidely Whiplash. Along with a collaborator, Chris created "The Munsters", a show that ran on CBS for two years and chronicled the twisted fortunes of a family of ghouls. Its popularity has remained endless and it still appears in syndicated reruns.

A King of Animation

They were the dominant force in kids cartoons, first in the movies and later in television. During the 1970's they accounted for 70% of the networks cartoon programming. **Joseph Barbera** was one-half of the much-celebrated partnership with Bill Hanna. Teaming together, they began by winning seven Oscars in the 1940's for their "Tom and Jerry" shorts.

When the MGM studio closed its animation department in the later 1950's, Hanna-Barbera moved to TV and created a series of hits in the following decade, beginning with "The Flintstones", which became the first animated series in prime time. They would go on to create the Jetsons, Yogi Bear, Scooby-Doo, Huckleberry Hound, Quick Draw McGraw, Top Cat and Jonny Quest. In all, they produced an astounding 300 series for network and syndicated television as well as adapting comic books and live-action series and creating theatrical features, direct-to-video releases and TV specials.

Shaped the Kansas City Sound

Jay McShann was in the thick of the action when Kansas City, Missouri was a hotbed of jazz activity in the late 1930's and early '40's. Along with Count Basie and Joe Turner, Jay (known as 'Hootie') helped to establish what came to be known as the Kansas City sound: a brand of jazz rooted in the blues, driven by riffs and marked by a powerful, but relaxed rhythmic pulse. In 1939 he expanded his group to big-band size and included teen saxophonist Charlie Parker as a member. Within a few years, Parker would emerge as the leader of the musical revolution known as bebop, but it was Jay who gave him the training he needed in the basics of swing and the blues. Jay was given a Pioneer Award from the Rhythm and Blues Foundation in 1996.

Scooby-Doo

It began as the final phrase in Frank Sinatra's song "Strangers in the Night" and became the animated lovable cowardly dog with an adventurous heart that captured a following for generations. **Iwao Takamoto** created Scooby-Doo after talking to a Great Dane breeder who had shown him pictures of how the dog stands: straight back and legs with a small chin. Based on the feedback, Iwao went in the opposite direction and created a character that had a hump back, bowed legs, big chin and the wrong color. Although he lacked formal training, Iwao was hired by Walt Disney Studios as an apprentice and assisted in the designs for "Cinderella",

"Peter Pan", "Lady and the Tramp" and "The Flintstones". Among other dogs he directly created was Astro from "The Jetsons".

Botanical Artist

She was known for painting flowers, herbs and insects in precise anatomical detail, using only live blossoms as models. House Beautiful, Life, Natural History and Smithsonian magazine published her illustrations. **Anne Ophelia Todd Dowden**'s work was exhibited at the Smithsonian, the New York Public Library and the Denver Museum of Art, among other places. Many of her artworks appeared in nature books for young readers. To research them, she collected weeds in railroad yards, pulled flowers apart from the inside and watched moths pollinate. Anne credited her first hand research with helping to bring her work alive and her watercolors garnered her the reputation as the country's leading botanical artist.

Transformed a Museum

When **Bradford Washburn** took over the New England Museum of Natural History it was little more than a dark repository of deteriorating stuffed animals and was described as a "grandmother's attic". Bradford said he got the job in 1939 because no one else wanted it. Over the next 41 years he would transform it into the renowned Boston Museum of Science. Relocated in 1951, it was the first to bring all science under one roof—natural, physical, applied and a planetarium. He felt the key was to bring science to life. Not stopping at being only a museum director, Bradford made eight first-recorded climbs of North American mountain peaks and mapped the Grand Canyon in the 1970's using his newly created high-resolution, large format aerial picture format that gave the Canyon a breathtaking clarity.

Poet a Minute

Beginning in the 1960's, **Maureen Cannon** rhymed observations about modern life in publications that included Good Housekeeping, Ladies Home Journal and Readers Digest. While still young, she would create strings of verses on the joys, real and imagined, of suburban life. It took years before she would be published in such diverse magazines as Playbill, Golf Digest, National Review and Progressive Grocer. In a forty-year period it was estimated that Maureen had more than 1,000 poems published, most of which were written in under one minute. Her topics ranged from the changing seasons, family life and holidays to aging, cell phones and uninvited guests.

I Love Lucy

One day **Bob Carroll, Jr.** and his writing partner were walking down the street in Hollywood and saw a pizza maker in the window tossing dough in the air. As writers for the "I Love Lucy" show, they called Lucille Ball and had her come down and learn how to spin the dough. The result was an episode created for the hit 1950's comedy show. Bob spent most of his 40-year comedy writing career thinking up new schemes and stunts for Lucy. Bob and two others were the sole writers for the first four seasons of "I Love Lucy", turning out 125 scripts. The Emmy Award-winning show was rated No. 1 for four of its six seasons and was never out of the top three. Bob would later write for four other situation comedy shows that starred Ms. Ball. He would also help to create "The Mothers-in-Law" television show and was a producer for the series "Alice" which won a Golden Globe. Bob received a lifetime writing achievement award from the Writers Guild of America in 1992.

Europe's Favorite American Choreographer

For thirty years, **Glen Tetley** was an integral part of the dance scene in Europe. Through his prolific creation of new works, he reversed a traditional pattern. In the past it was typical for the United States to take its ballet signals from Europe, but Glen introduced and integrated American modern-dance movements into European choreography. An original member of the Joffrey Ballet in 1956, he worked less with contemporary dance troupes he helped to mold in London and the Netherlands and became associated, in the 1970's, with major ballet companies in Britain, Australia, Germany and Denmark. Today, choreographers commonly mix modern dance and ballet, but Glen combined ballet's celebrated moves with the artistry of the Martha Graham dance form when it was considered less acceptable to do so.

West Indian Parade

1920's Harlem in New York City held the original events that would, decades later, evolve into the West Indian American Day Carnival. The carnival left the Savoy, Renaissance and Audubon ballrooms in 1965 and headed to Brooklyn where **Carlos Lezama** led the carnival association for 35 years. A few hundred people participated the first two years it was held near his home in Crown Heights in Brooklyn. By the third year he had obtained a permit to hold the parade along the much-traveled Eastern Parkway and the crowds swelled. By 2001, Carlos' last year as coordinator, the parade drew an estimated two million parade watchers for the annual Labor Day carnival that included 10,000 marchers, 42 bands and 30 floats. The parade included whimsical depictions of ocean life, outer space and flowers of the world. Some marchers would dance around in grass skirts, leopard-skin warrior costumes and as winged butterflies.

Waterloo Village

In the 1820's, there was a thriving commercial center serving the traffic along an industrial canal in northern New Jersey. By the 1960's, some 30 buildings, including a gristmill, canal house, tavern, general store and church, were falling apart, the relics of a bygone era. **Percival Leach** and a business partner bought and restored the village building by building and turned in into a tourist attraction. Led by guides in period gowns and bonnets, visitors could watch a blacksmith hammering out iron rivets and cupboard latches, a potter shaping clay jugs on a treadle wheel and women hooking rugs, dipping candles or weaving cloth on looms. Furnishings dating from the Federal to the Victorian periods filled the old homes. In Waterloo Village, you could walk through history in one afternoon.

National Ballet of Canada

She moved to Canada from London at the age of 29 at the invitation of some Toronto arts patrons and members of the business community who wanted to form a ballet company. **Celia Franca** was known in England as a strong, dramatic dancer who had performed leading roles in London during the 1940's. She found work as a clerk in a Toronto department store and, less than a year later, founded the National Ballet of Canada which made its debut in the auditorium of the store where Celia worked. During her 24 years as its artistic director, she brought in works by Europe's leading choreographers, including Rudolf Nureyev.

Funk Brother

They were the sound behind the phenomenal success of Motown records in the 1960's. The Funk Brothers were the studio musicians who played on numerous blockbuster hits from the era. **Joe Hunter** was the first person hired by the legendary Berry Gordy, Jr. who was Motown's founder. Joe had backed up such acts as Smokey Robinson and the Miracles in the late 50's when Gordy took Joe on as his first bandleader. Joe's piano work was integral on Martha and the Vandella's "Heat Wave" and "Come and Get These Memories" as well as Marvin Gaye's "Pride and Joy". The Funk Brothers played on "My Guy", "I Head it Through the Grapevine", "Baby Love", "Signed, Sealed, Delivered" and "The Tears of a Clown", to name a few. The Funk Brothers played on more number one records than the Beatles, Elvis, The Rolling Stones and The Beach Boys combined.

The Keebler Elf

Ernie, the animated Keebler elf seen on television commercials, had a human voice behind the cartoon character. It was **Walker Edmiston** who portrayed Ernie in the cookie promotional ads. He spent a good part of his career as a voiceover artist when he was also heard on The Flintstones, The Smurfs and Spider-Man as well as several other shows. When not behind the microphone, he seemed as if he had a guest star role in most of the television shows of the 50's through the 80's: The Waltons, Little House on the Prairie, Falcon Crest, Knots Landing, Dallas, Gunsmoke, Columbo, Bonanza, Mission: Impossible, Mannix, Star Trek, The Big Valley, Green Acres, The Bob Newhart Show and The Mary Tyler Moore Show, just to name a few.

Abstract Painter

Color field painting is identified by its emphasis on the paint being applied to a flat surface. It stays away from creating the illusion of depth and noticeable brush strokes, but concentrates on the vibrancy of the color alone. **Jules Olitski** became a leading advocate of Color Field in the 1960's and it was said that his paintings looked like colors that had been sprayed into the air and stuck to the canvas. He was very prolific and had more than 150 one-man exhibitions worldwide. In 1969 he became only the third living person to have a one-man show at the Metropolitan Museum of Art in New York City. His paintings remain on display at the Met as well as the Guggenheim and Modern in New York as well as many other museums.

The Sound of Tap Dancing

He called it Tap-Tronics, a way of radically changing and expanding the sound of tap-dancing. **Alfred Desio** started the idea in 1982 while he was doing a radio promotion for a dance festival. The radio engineer put his taps through a delay. It became obvious that by taping the sound of the foot hitting the floor and controlling it, you could create rhythms that resembled music rather than the accustomed rat-a-tat tap sounds. A few years later Alfred brought what he called his Zapped Taps to 6,000 people in a performance for Lincoln Center Out of Doors in New York City. The 1989 film "Tap" used a version of Trap-Tronics that was performed by tap star Gregory Hines.

Livened Up the Planetarium Experience

Working in a basement studio with an airbrush, **Helmut Wimmer** produced hundreds of paintings on cardboard sheets that were transferred onto high-resolution slides. The result was vivid depictions of twirling planets, glowing comets, pulsing nebulas and black holes that fascinated thousands of visitors under the dome of the Hayden Planetarium in New York City. Inserted into as many as 200 projectors on the perimeter of the dome, his images served as a magnificent view of seamless panoramas of the cosmos. Helmut's artwork allowed generations of visitors to transport themselves from Earth to the surface of a star, the moon or a black hole. His painting of an early image of a black hole in 1974 made the cover of The New York Times Magazine and numerous science publications.

Theater for Children

Theaterworks/USA was started by **Jay Harnick** in 1961with the intention of expanding children's theater beyond shows with dancing vegetables. The company attracted top talent as they produced historical plays for kids. It helped start the careers of many actors, including an Oscar winner for Best Actor, F. Murray Abraham, and one of television's most recognizable characters, Fonzie, played by Henry Winkler. The company has toured shows in 49 states and Canada, playing to millions of children every year, and had put together a repertory of 117 musicals and plays. Jay served as artistic director for nearly forty years.

Opera Composer

His first opera was written before he was 11 and was recognized as the most-often-performed living composer of opera. **Gian Carlo Menotti** made the art form understandable and enjoyable for many people who otherwise had no interest. In all, he composed 25 operas, almost all in English and usually staged his own works. He won two Pulitzer Prizes, which included "The Saint of Bleecker Street" in 1954 that was the only Broadway production to earn the cultural "triple crown" of the Pulitzer, the New York Drama Critics Circle Award and New York Music Critics Award. His Christmas classic, "Amahl and the Night Visitors", was performed more than 600 times since it was created for television in 1951. Gian Carlo also founded the Festival of Two Worlds, the long-running summer music festival that began in 1958 in Spoleto, Italy that he directed for more than 40 years. An American offshoot of Spoleto was established in Charleston, South Carolina in 1977.

Hit Songwriter

Ray Evans and his writing partner, Jay Livingston, wrote some of the most enduring songs in the great American songbook. With Ray providing the lyrics and Jay the music, they wrote songs for dozens of movies during a ten-year period from 1945 to '55. They produced three Oscar winning songs, "Buttons and Bows", "Mona Lisa" and "Que Sera, Sera". Possibly their best known song was the Christmas classic "Silver Bells" which has been recorded by nearly 150 artists and sold more than 160 million copies. In all, their songs have sold almost 500 million copies. After feature films, they moved on to write the themes for the popular television shows "Bonanza" and "Mr. Ed".

Fluxus

This art form came from a group of international artists, writers and musicians who began working together to stage happenings and performances in the early 1960's. It never defined itself as an art movement because it was anti-authoritarian in nature and gave birth to video art, performance art and conceptual art. Its first performance took place in Weisbaden, Germany in 1962. **Emmett Williams** was an American poet who transposed words into visual art that made him one of the founding artists of Fluxus. He was living in Germany when he began writing to the originator of Fluxus. Emmett performed his poetry that was referred to as a score.

Changed Las Vegas

Around 1950, the Mary Kaye Trio was winding up its first engagement in the main showroom of the Last Frontier on what would become known as the Las Vegas Strip when the owner wanted to keep the group at the hotel. Lead singer **Mary Kaye** suggested that a stage be built in the bar area that they could call a 'lounge'. The name stuck and the term "lounge act" made its way into the vocabulary of Las Vegas shows. The trio performed between 1AM and 6AM on the newly enclosed stage and turned Vegas into a 24-hour town. They worked an average of 36 weeks a year, often appearing at the Sahara and Tropicana hotels. Celebrities often took in the act, including Elvis who watched from backstage.

Danish Furniture

He considered himself as a cabinetmaker, but everyone saw him as a remarkable designer of primarily furniture chairs. **Hans Wegner** rose to attention as one of a few Danish designers who produced fresh sculptural and organic modern furniture. He combined the old time cabinetmaker traditions of high craftsmanship, quality and comfort with the modern qualities of simplicity and graphic beauty. His two best-known chair designs were introduced in 1949. One was the Wishbone chair, with a Y-shaped back split and curved back and armrest, an idea he got from a child's chair made in China that he had seen. His other creation was known as the Chair, or the Round Chair. With a caned seat and a back and armrests that were made of one continuous circle of wood, it gained recognition when it was the chair selected by presidential candidates John Kennedy and Richard Nixon for their first historic televised debate in 1960.

Boys Choir of Harlem

The group was founded in a church basement in 1968 by **Walter Turnbull**. Starting out at 20 boys, the choir eventually blossomed into 150 strong and included a 600-student school that offered a full academic program from grades 4 through 12. Walter was working toward a doctorate when he started the choir as an after-school music program. The boys would go on to sing for presidents and popes and were celebrated around the world as a symbol of the success that can be brought out of the ghetto. A typical performance would range from the classical music of Handel to spirituals, jazz and pop. Beyond musical training, the choir each year provides educational and personal counseling to hundreds of inner-city youth from ages 9 to 19.

Scholar of Comic Strips

He said he loved cartooning because it was accessible to all people. **Jay Kennedy** was known as a scholar of comics, especially 1960's-era underground comic strips. In what he called his dream job, he was an editor at King Features and helped to revive the old "Prince Valiant" strip as well as popularizing "Curtis", "Mutts" and "Zits". Jay would routinely spend months before a strip's debut by mapping out characters and story lines to determine whether the artist had the required vision and staying power. He wrote articles about the history of cartooning and profiled cartoonists and contemporary comics for several magazines. Jay introduced a website, dailyink.com, which made available more than 70 current and vintage strips.

Innovative Album Covers

He was an artist in a now obsolete format, using the 12-inch square album cover as his canvas for pictures that varied widely in appearance. **Joel Brodsky** photographed nearly 400 album covers for a diverse group of musicians that included Kiss, Gladys Knight and the Pips, Aretha Franklin, Jim Morrison, Carly Simon, B. B. King and Barry Manilow. It was said that what famed photographer Annie Leibovitz does today Joel was doing 30 years ago. Five of his photos became album covers for the legendary 60's group the Doors and Joel received a Grammy nomination for the group's debut album. By the 70's, he received attention for designing and photographing a series of seven album covers for the Ohio Players, none of which showed the band.

Rockefeller Center Christmas Tree

The tradition began humbly in 1931 when construction workers put up a small tree on a building in mid-town Manhattan in the complex that became known as Rockefeller Center. Two years later a formal tree lighting ceremony began and over the years it turned into a national event. **Marc Torsilieri**'s landscaping company had developed a reputation for sensitivity in moving large trees and was approached to handle the annual centerpiece tree. A Norway spruce was always required because of its brisk growth. Each fall Marc and his team would scour primarily the Northeast to find the perfect tree although, in the past, they did find the right match in Canada and Ohio. Once the right tree is found, they tie up the 85-footer, weighing eight tons and measuring 40 feet wide, and tie back every branch to make the trip through Manhattan. Each year's tree is decorated with 30,000 lights with five miles of wire, with a star on top that weighs 550 pounds.

A Wizard of the Kiln

Their work elevated ceramics from a decorative art to a fine art. After **Otto Natzler**'s wife and artistic partner, Gertrude, died several decades ago, he carried on their work alone Through the years, he developed more than 1,000 glazes for pottery, many with a glossy, silken look. The shapes were in the form of craters, volcanoes, ocean bottoms, mountain gaps, molten pools and crystals exploding into the shape of a star. Over seven decades, their work was displayed in numerous gallery shows and are permanently housed in such world class facilities as the New York Museum of Modern Art, the Metropolitan Museum in New York, the Art Institute in Chicago and the Victoria and Albert Museum in London.

Mature Photographer

She bought her first camera at the age of 62 and the initial three rolls she developed turned out black because **Ruth Gilbert** didn't know how to load the film. She studied a series of Time-Life books on the technical aspects of picture taking and within a decade her work was being touted by the most prominent photographers in the field. With help, her photos were published in an influential European photography magazine and several selections were placed in France's prestigious Bibliotheque Nationale, the French version of the US Library of Congress. Ruth's projects were also shown around the world in private galleries or museums.

The Zydeco Sound

At first he played the button accordion, an instrument with a family tradition. **Bois Sec Ardoin** came from southwestern Louisiana, an area whose traditional songs and tunes were shared by both the black and white population. For fifty years he traded quick-fingered passages with his fiddler partner on some of the oldest known Creole tunes and infused Cajun waltzes along with the blues. It was known as "la musique Creole" and would later pick up the name of "zydeco", a style that is still heard in South Louisiana dance halls. Bois Sec was credited with brining Creole music into the mainstream when he played at the 1966 Newport folk festival. Twenty years later he received the National Heritage Fellowship from the National Endowment for the Arts, the highest American award for work in the traditional arts.

Popularized Tatooing

With vivid images of dragons, daggers, cartoon characters and crests that he distributed to tattoo parlors around the world, **Michael Malone** standardized the art of tattoo making. He was noted for "the flash", 11-by-17 inch posters on tattoo parlor walls that show up to a dozen images that clients can select. Most parlors had hand drawn their designs which were primarily bad because the designers were not very talented. Michael was known for blending Asian and Western images with an occasional dash of humor. He was the first to distribute flash sheets featuring Hawaiian designs from the time before the missionaries arrived in the 19th century, with arm, leg and wrist bands of interlocked triangles, diamonds and arrows.

The Master of Tap

For nearly 60 years, **Henry LeTang** maintained a internationally renowned studio in New York City that taught the leading lights of Broadway and Hollywood how to tap dance. If a show featured tap dancing, it was highly likely that Henry had a hand in its production. He choreographed some of Broadway's best-known musicals and was a Tony award winner. The list of performers he taught reads like a Who's Who of 20th century show business: Debbie Allen, Harry Belafonte, Milton Berle, Lola Falana, the Hines brothers, Lena Horne, Betty Hutton, Bette Middler, Chita Rivera and Ben Vereen, among many others.

Studio Pottery

Mary Scheier combined simple glazes with her thin pots to create elegant vessels that gained her much acclaim in the field. She was a pioneer of the modern studio pottery movement and was recognized for the lightness of her forms. Mary made functional pottery and small sculptures out of clay that she and her husband dug out for themselves while opting not to order refined clay from a laboratory. Among her creations were pieces that resembled pottery from the Sung dynasty, an era she greatly admired.

Nigerian Musician

People in Nigeria look to music to soothe the daily challenges of life. **Chief Stephen Osita Osadebe** was considered a titan of the African popular music known as 'highlife', a celebratory music where the juncture of high-society bands and traditional African rhythms mesh together. His 1984 hit, "Osondi Owendi" was the biggest selling record in the history of Nigeria. He was known as the "Doctor of Hypertension" as a reference to the healing power of his music. Stephen wrote more than 500 songs and prided himself on being a composer of music and lyrics. He felt that if you couldn't compose your own song you didn't deserve to be a musician.

Roy Rogers of Mexico

The remark was that neither his singing nor his voice made **Antonio Aguilar** memorable, but it was his character and the way he treated musicians and interacted with the audience. In a career that spanned six decades, he made more than 160 records and 100 films, often portraying roles as a fearless champion of the poor in dramas with revolutionary themes. He was one of the first Mexican artists to develop a fan base among Mexican immigrants in the United States and to also engage non-Latino audiences in his performances. Several of his classic songs are still sung throughout Mexico, often in cantinas and at parties, and help to invoke the melancholy of life.

Black Theater

When he traveled to theaters across America the message was always the same: black run theaters were hurting for money, good management and audiences. **Larry Hamlin** decided to take matters into his own hands by forming a festival in Winston-Salem, NC with the intention of bringing together theater companies so they could learn from one another. It was referred to as the "holy ground" of black theater, a not-to-be-missed event that offers networking, information and exposure at a place where high-quality plays and culture could be enjoyed by large gatherings. Since its founding in 1989, the festival is held every two years and has grown to include 40 productions, an audience of 60,000 and an international lineup of artists that has included Denzel Washington and Sidney Poitier.

Book Art

Outside the artistic community, book art is sometimes confused with illustration which is art that accompanies text and helps tell a story. With **Gloria Helfgott**, the book itself is both the work of art and the story. In book art, words and pages are not mandatory and the artwork bears little resemblance to the traditional definition of a book. Gloria transformed her studio into a classroom for students and her work helped to define the genre for audiences throughout the United States. Her book art can be found at the Brooklyn Museum, the Victoria and Albert Museum in London, the Museum of Modern Art in New York City and Stanford University.

The Father of African Film

Ousmane Sembene took up filmmaking because he believed that cinema could reach a wider and more diverse audience than literature. His debut feature, "Black Girl", in 1965 is commonly referred to as the first African film and combined a realistic script with the elements of traditional African storytelling. In all, Ousmane directed ten features and numerous short films. The central themes of his work showed the tensions between tradition and the present and contrasted newly independent African nations with their former colonial rulers. Both drama and comedy were played out while focusing on the lives of ordinary people, primarily women. He was a winner at both the Cannes and Venice film festivals.

Art Perception

How we interpret art and, by extension, the world was the focal point for **Rudolph Arnheim**. As a psychologist, philosopher and critic, he was absorbed with the way humans experience the sensory world. He critiqued painting, photography, film, architecture, radio soap operas and television. Among the questions he raised: what happens in the mind when we see a work of art? Does a work of art represent reality or does it shape our interpretation of reality? Rudolph arrived at the conclusion that through the acts of seeing, hearing and touching, we are able to make sense of the world around us.

Multi-Dimensions

Called posterization, it's a technique that converted black-and-white or color photographs into a series of three separate negatives, each designated for a different color. They were then printed together, each slightly off the mark. The result appeared to be multidimensional. **Martin Weber** invented a number of typographic and graphic techniques, but none was more popular than the creation that made two-dimension pictures seem to leap off the page. It was used frequently during the 1960's by underground poster artists to give their artwork a psychedelic look. Back in 1942, Martin invented and patented a photographic device that could change the appearance of gothic lettering, by expanding, compressing or blowing it up. The device helped to start a trend in special effects lettering.

Hummel Sculptor

With their compact bodies, chubby cheeks, enormous shoes and sentimental appeal, Hummel figurines are instantly recognizable. They have been issued in more than 1,000 styles and can range in price from $100 up to $4,000. Inspired by the drawings of a Bavarian woman named Berta Hummel, the figures have been created since 1935 and have sold more than 20 million around the world. **Gerhard Skrobek** was the master sculptor at the Goebel porcelain factory in Rodental, Germany where the Hummels are made. He updated classic designs of the past and oversaw the production of new figures. Gerhard was also a roving ambassador for Hummel and traveled throughout Europe and the United States where he was met by thousands of enthusiastic admirers of the figurines.

Innovative Film Director

Coming from a generation of rule breakers, **Michelangelo Antonioni** was one of the most subversive and revered movie directors. He rose to prominence in the 1950's when filmmaking was considered to be an intellectual pursuit. He challenged moviegoers with a focus on vague characters and a disdain for the typical plot. Many of his cuts, scene lengths and camera movements were highly unique. Michelangelo raised questions in his films that were never answered and had characters act in self-destructive ways. "Blowup" was his most recognized work, a 1966 movie based in London about a fashion photographer who believes he has witnessed a murder. It earned Michelangelo Oscar nominations for best director and screenplay.

The Master Filmmaker

His films dealt with pain and torment, desire and religion, evil and love. **Ingmar Bergman** made 50 movies over more than 40 years while centering his work on two great themes—the relationship between the sexes and the dynamic between people and God. He found bleakness and despair as well as comedy and hope in exploring the human condition. He won Oscars three times for best foreign language film—"The Virgin Spring (1960)", "Through the Glass Darkly (1961)" and "Fanny and Alexander (1983)". Ingmar was awarded the prestigious Irving Thalberg award in 1970 for his body of work.

Punk Rock

The club was an open door to any band willing to take a chance. Situated in the Lower East Side of New York City in an area know as the Bowery, CBGB's was run by **Hilly Kristal** and welcomed thousands of bands, for nearly 33 years, to perform their own music. Such innovative groups as the Ramones, Patti Smith, Blondie, Talking Heads and Sonic Youth perfected their sound in what became known as the cradle of punk and art-rock music. The guesstimate was that about 30 bands a week made their way through the club, a total of nearly 50,000 over the decades. With stickers and taped-up fliers lining the walls from years past, CBGB's became a tourist draw as both a relic of rock history and a living museum of graffiti.

Smooth Jazz

Years before it was fashionable to do so, **Jon Lucien** used his rich, expressive baritone to sing over quiet arrangements and swaying rhythms to set the tone for what became known as the sound of smooth jazz. With a suave, romantic delivery, he never seemed to break a sweat. With signature songs "Would You Believe in Me", "Lady Love" and "Dindi", he still was never able to get a Top 40 hit. As an original songwriter and performer, Jon made music that wasn't easy to categorize and was only able to see success when the smooth jazz format came along in the late 1980's and '90's.

Activist Writer

The output was modest: about four-dozen stories in three volumes. But the work was widely praised by critics for the pitch-perfect dialogue that explored the lives of women in their daily routines. **Grace Paley** was among the earliest American writers to do that, focusing on mostly Jewish New Yorkers who were primarily single mothers. Her stories were marked with their minute attention to language that made them a delight when read aloud. In 1993, Grace won the equivalent of the Pulitzer Prize for short-story writing by receiving the Rea Award. She was called a pure short story writer, a natural to the form in the way that rarely gifted athletes are said to be natural.

Bebop

He was not the first drummer to play this type of music, but **Max Roach** quickly established himself as both the most imaginative percussionist in modern jazz and the most influential. Layering rhythms on top of rhythms, he paid as much attention to the song's melody as to its beat. Bebop had its roots in the jazz tradition, but it was unique in that the rhythm was jagged and unpredictable and its harmonies more advanced. As an instrumentalist, Max brought the drum to the front of the stage and made each element of the drum into a special instrument. From the time of his recording debut in 1944, he showed a mastery of this new style of drumming and positioned himself as a cutting edge member of the new bebop fraternity.

Keeper of the Mouse

The nickname **Ralph Kent** earned came from being one of Mickey Mouse's handlers, concerning him with maintaining the cartoon character's wholesome image. Ralph would train other artists to draw Mickey the same way and he personally selected which merchandise would carry his image. He designed what still remains a memorable collectible, a limited-edition adult Mickey Mouse watch that was given to top company executives in 1965. Ralph was also behind the signature and for a period of time he was one of the few people who were authorized to sign on Mickey's behalf. When he retired in 2004 he was named a Disney legend and honored with a window on Main Street.

Playhouse 90

This CBS television show debuted in 1956 and won eleven Emmy's in its first two seasons under the guidance of **Martin Manulis** who served as the sole producer. He would oversee more than 60 segments, including every one of those first two years in what was considered to be television's golden age of drama. The program aired live for 90 minutes for 30 weeks a year, adapting works from writers such as Hemingway, Odets, Faulkner and Fitzgerald. In a poll of television editors by Variety magazine in 1970, it was voted the greatest TV series of all time. In 2002, TV Guide ranked Playhouse 90 at Number 33 in its list of the 50 greatest shows ever.

Fiber Art

During the late 1950's and early '60's, arts and crafts were seen as mutually exclusive. **Lenore Tawney** united the two by combining several different techniques such as plain weave, gauze weave, slit tapestry and open-warp weaving to invent large, abstract and free-hanging sculptural forms. Many of the postcard collages she made over the years had fragile objects attached to their surfaces, including seashells, feathers and the tiny bones of birds. She never considered a piece finished until it traveled through the mail. It was not enclosed in an envelope, but was taken to the post office to be hand stamped and left with a clerk. Lenore's work has been in the collections of the Museum of Modern Art, the Metropolitan Museum of Art, the Art Institute of Chicago and the Cooper-Hewitt National Design Museum.

Narrative Quilts

In the early days, she learned that quilts could be made from scraps of anything, an aunt had made hers from feed and flour sacks and stuffed them with cotton from the fields where she worked. **Nora Ezell** already had a well earned reputation in the world of quilting when the Birmingham, Alabama Civil Rights Institute commissioned her in the early 1990's to produce quilts that recognized the sacrifices of civil rights workers in their state. Among the images she created was the Edmund Pettis Bridge, site of the 1965 attack by police on marchers; Martin Luther King, Jr. writing his Letter from a Birmingham jail in 1953; Rosa Parks refusing to give up her seat on a Montgomery bus in 1955 and a panel commemorating the 1963 bombing of a Baptist church in Birmingham that killed schoolchildren. Nora's works are now in collections around the world, including the American Folk Art Museum in New York City.

Female Elvis

She was one of the few women to make a mark in the masculine, raw-edged music that would become known as rockabilly. Winning nearly every talent contest she entered, by the age of 11 **Janis Martin** was being featured on a country music radio show and began to take to the road. By 16, she had recorded the song "Will You, Willyum" that propelled her into a national tour while becoming one of the first Americans singers to barnstorm through Europe. With the approval of her RCA label mate, Elvis Presley, Janis was called "the female Elvis". Another hit, "Let's Elope, Baby" rang true to life with Janis getting married at age 15. She was dropped by her record label and faded into the backlight.

Children's Classic

The book was rejected by 26 publishers before it was finally accepted. "A Wrinkle in Time" would win the John Newberry Medal as the best children's book of 1963, sell 8 million copies and go through 69 printings. **Madeleine L'Engle** was called one of the truly important writers of juvenile fiction in decades. The book began with the often-mimicked phrase "it was a dark and stormy night" and used time travel to send the book's main character, Meg Murry, and her psychic brother to rescue their scientist father from a planet controlled by the Dark Thing. The book used concepts that Madeleine said she had taken from Einstein's theory of relativity and Planck's quantum theory. She had frequently stated that children's literature is too difficult for adults to understand.

BUSINESS

The Wax Museum

He had dinner one night in 1964 with the owner of a traveling circus that included a collection of wax figures. The following day, **Spoony Singh** got on a plane to Hollywood, found a spot near Grauman's Chinese Theatre and signed a 20-year lease on a 15,000 square foot building. It opened the following year with a half-mile long line the first day waiting to pay $1.50 to see the wax figures of Hollywood's biggest stars and the world's most recognizable people. At a given time, nearly 200 figures are on display and characters change with the popular tastes. The head and hands are wax, but the bodies are made of fiberglass. It's estimated than more than 8 million people have made their way through the museum in the last four decades.

The Ultimate Free Market Thinker

Milton Friedman was considered a leading economic thinker of the 20th century and was a prime force in moving countries toward less government and more reliance on individual responsibility. As an economic conservative, he led the challenge to the revered theories of John Maynard Keynes, the British economist, who felt that the government had a duty to bring the economy through tough times and prevent the good times from spiraling out of control into runaway inflation. Milton believed the government should keep its hands off the economy and let the free market take care of matters. A long time professor at the University of Chicago, he never held an official government position, but he had as much of an impact on the government as anyone. Predicting the arrival of stagflation, a combination of rising unemployment and rising inflation that had been unknown before, won Milton the 1976 Nobel Prize in Economics.

LexisNexis

At first many lawyers refused to use **H. Donald Wilson**'s new software because they regarded computer work as a secretarial function. He had created a business plan, in the 1960's, to capitalize on an engineer's invention to search a text for certain words or phrases. In order to gain acceptance, he gave law students almost free access to the electronic files of court decisions. By the time they graduated, the students were pushing law firms to adopt its use. A major step forward came when H. Donald arranged for clerks at the Supreme Court to use the system and wound up finding cases more quickly than the manual method. The database became known as LexisNexis and was a boon to not only law firms, but businesses, libraries and the news industry.

Ice Cream that Everybody Loves

The company was started in the 1920's by **Rose Mattus**' husband who would deliver the family's homemade ice cream to neighborhood stores in the South Bronx by horse-drawn wagon. Come 1960, when Rose was sitting on their living room couch one night, she came up with the Danish sounding name "Haagen Dazs" which, by the way, does not mean anything in Danish. At the time, most supermarket ice cream was made with artificial flavoring and nonfat dry milk. Rose and her husband began using egg yolks, real cream, Belgian chocolate, vanilla beans from Madagascar and Columbian coffee. She would take free samples to bodegas and grocery stores to stimulate interest. When the company was sold to Pillsbury in 1983, sales were $115 million a year.

A Mail Campaign Second to None

In never appeared in newspapers or magazines and was never shown on television nor heard on the radio. It was a simple two-page letter that was a subscription pitch for The Wall Street Journal. **Martin Conroy** wrote: "On a beautiful late spring afternoon, twenty-five years ago, two young men graduated from the same college. They were very much alike, these two young men. Both had been better than average students, both were personable and both—as young college graduates are—were filled with ambitious dreams for the future. Recently, these men returned to their college for their 24th reunion." Written quite plainly with the hint of "what ever happened to?" the letter became widely recognized as the class of direct-mail marketing. The letter was sent to millions of potential subscribers over a 28-year period, longer than any other direct mail effort ever made anywhere.

Made CBS into the Tiffany Network

Although he spent his career in the shadow of a broadcasting legend, **Frank Stanton** led CBS for 28 years and helped to create the most prestigious communications company in the world. Alongside William Paley, Frank was a central figure in the development of television broadcasting in the United States. He pioneered efforts to analyze audience feedback on programming, rolled out the block program format, bundled similar programs together during the day, persuaded Congress to suspend the equal-time rule for presidential debates and opened the door for today's familiar format of debates between the leading candidates. He had to pull the plug on the network's quiz shows in the 1950's after it was revealed that several programs had manipulated the results. Frank came to be regarded as broadcasting's foremost statesman.

Magic Noodles

A few years after the end of World War II, **Momofuku Ando** was walking through the rubble strewn streets of Osaka, Japan and saw people standing outside in the shivering cold waiting for their turn to buy noodles. Turning back centuries of tradition which held that noodles had to be cooked fresh, Momofuku created the instant noodle that could be dried, packaged, and reheated in a bowl of boiling water in just three minutes. He began exporting his tasty, inexpensive and easy to make noodles to the United States in 1970 and labeled them Cup Noodles. Today, the company now produces 16 flavors, including six varieties of chicken as well as shrimp, vegetable and spicy chili. Momofuku's once small company turned into a $3 billion a year multinational corporation with 29 subsidiaries in 11 countries.

Mayor of Broadway

It was considered to be one of the world's most famous restaurants, a New York City institution as central to the life of the Broadway theater as its actors, agents and critics. Sardi's restaurant was the club, dining hall, lounge, post office, saloon and marketplace for theater people. **Vincent Sardi, Jr.** kept it all together as owner of the West 44th Street eatery. Taking over from his father (the original owner) in 1947, Vincent would attend every Broadway show so he could easily recognize his many patrons. He was known to seat a hungry actor near a producer who might have a solid role that needed to be cast. He would carry out-of-work actors and let them run up tabs until their finances improved. At one point, Vincent had 600 such accounts. In its heyday in the 1960's, a new Broadway show was constantly opening and a line would form down the street with theatergoers, theater insiders and the curious hoping to get a table to watch the drama unfold as the first reviews came off the printing press and were rushed to Sardi's at midnight for the cast to read.

Those Comfy Slippers

During World War II, the Firestone Tire and Rubber Company invented a material that was to be used as a helmet liner for tank crewmen. The intention of **Florence Melton**'s trip to Firestone in the late 1940's was to buy their foam rubber to make shoulder pads for women's clothing. On the way home, she told her husband they should also use the foam to make slippers. The first women's version was sold in 1947 and was followed by men's slippers in the 1950's. From the start, the slippers were available in a range of fabrics and styles, including slip-ons and closed-heels. Known as Deerfoams, they are made of washable terrycloth or velour and come in a variety of colors. Some have backs, some have straps, some have open toes and some have tassels. All versions share the same half-inch thick soft-foam rubber insole. Last year alone, 25 million pair was sold.

NASDAQ

Electronic stock trading was introduced in 1971 by **Gordon Macklin**. Bulky cathode ray terminals allowed thousands of stockbrokers across the country to buy and sell shares over the computer rather than manually over the counter. Sales could be executed just by the push of a button. Prior to the National Association of Securities Dealers Automated Quotations systems (NASDAQ), every market had a physical location. Gordon was able to bring traders together electronically into one market. Initially, only the shares of smaller companies used the new format, but over time much larger companies, such as Microsoft and Apple, came on board. Today, all markets, including the New York Stock Exchange, are becoming predominantly electronic markets.

Set Newspaper Standards

Back in the heyday of newspapers, nearly 90% of Americans subscribed in the 1950's. Most staffs just threw together words and pictures because they knew the paper would become obsolete within hours. Magazines, by contrast, had a longer shelf life and were designed to make an attractive appearance. **Edmund Arnold** helped to implement changes that are now standard in newspapers: bigger type and six columns of print with a more legible appearance than the old eight columns. He pioneered the use of a layout in which stories were packed in squares and not long, haphazard columns that seemed to jump over the page. Edmund also pushed for photographs that helped to enhance the story and not just appear as a meaningless decoration. In all, he designed or redesigned hundreds of newspaper, including The Chicago Tribune, The Christian Science Monitor, Newsday and The Boston Globe.

Auctioned Classic Cars

Before each auction, **Russell Kruse** would sing "Back Home Again in Indiana", even if he weren't in the state. With his farm flooded out for two straight years, Russell headed to a two-week school to learn how to auctioneer. It took another twenty years, in 1971, to come up with the idea of selling classic cars at auction. The chamber of commerce had asked him to help raise money for its annual show that honored the companies who once made cars in Auburn, Indiana. 17,000 people showed up and it marked the start of an auction market for classic vehicles. Among his auctioned cars was a 1933 Duesenberg Victoria once owned by Greta Garbo, John Lennon's 1956 Bentley and a Batmobile. Today, the company Russell founded now holds 150 antique automobile auctions all over the world, selling more than $200 million worth of cars each year.

Matchbox Cars

A gifted casting engineer, **John Odell** fashioned a tiny model of a road roller for his daughter to take to school in a match box after she kept scaring her schoolmates by storing spiders in the small compartment. Within two years, nearly 20 vehicles were being made based on John's designs. The toys quickly spread to the United States where they sold for 49 cents in the mid-1950's. John would visit automakers around the world to copy their creations. The carmakers actually appreciated the free publicity and permitted him to move forward. A milestone was reached in 1953 when he sold more than a million copies of the coronation coach of Queen Elizabeth II.

Grandfather of Specialty Coffee

In the 1960's, just about everybody was drinking coffee out of a can. **Alfred Peet** was the guru of the gourmet coffee revolution when he opened a store in Berkeley, California and began serving a dark roasted cup. He was rooted in the European tradition and paid attention to the preparation, the ritual and understanding of how beans were grown. It was said that Alfred was the big bang of cultured coffee, it all began with him. His single retail coffee bean store would eventually blossom into a public company with 150 stores in 10 states. Alfred inspired a generation of coffee entrepreneurs. In 1971, a store opened in Seattle with coffee roasted by Alfred's company. Its name was Starbucks.

The Beer Hunter

Also known as "The Bard of Beer", **Michael Jackson** was a leading authority on beer and his criticism helped restore interest in breweries and sparked the microbrewery movement in the United States. When it came to beer he was known as the single most influential person in the world. His 1977 book, "The World Guide to Beer", said that there were about 40 breweries in the US producing boring beer. Thirty years later there are 1,440 breweries in the country with nearly 1,400 small, independent companies known as craft brewers. Michael was the first one to take an academic approach to the culture of beer by looking at people's habits, traditions, the taste of beer and the styles in which it was brewed. He spent half the year traveling and visited as many as 200 brewers a year. It was estimated that Michael had sampled 10,000 beers during his career.

Nautilus Machines

It was born out of frustration. In 1948, **Arthur Jones** became irritated when the exercise equipment at the YMCA where he was living failed to give him the physical lift he was seeking. For nearly 20 years he tinkered around until coming up with the Blue Monster, the first name he gave to a Nautilus machine. When it was introduced at a fitness competition, weightlifting was a narrow specialized activity populated with hard-core bodybuilders who worked out in darkly lit gyms. At first, the reception was less than enthusiastic, but from the early 70's to the mid-80's Nautilus cornered the conditioning business in America with stylish facilities popping up across the country accompanied by the first personal trainers who would guide exercisers through their workouts.

EDUCATION

Made Math Simple

It can be quite intimidating trying to learn new math concepts. **Paul Halmos** once said that mathematics is "almost like being in touch with God. God is keeping secrets from us and it's fun to learn some of those secrets". His work focused on such challenging areas as algebraic logic, measure theory and the naïve set theory. Paul was also identified with probability theory, the study of randomness under differing conditions and operator theory. Despite its confusing nature, Paul was able to express complex ideas in a concise fashion by simplifying both written and verbal math and becoming an early advocate for using the tombstone symbol to signify the end of a proof. The symbol acts as a punctuation mark and is sometimes referred to as a 'halmos'.

The Multicultural Historian

He was one of the key people who invented the field of American cultural history. **Lawrence Levine**'s elegant scholarship bolstered arguments for multiculturalism in higher education. During a long career on the faculty at the University of California Berkeley, his books challenged the conventional wisdom in subjects ranging from Shakespeare to slave songs to the college curriculum. His most critically acclaimed book "Black Culture and Consciousness" showed how slaves had developed their own culture within the confines of slavery. In another work, he rejected the idea that a "classical" college course load had ever existed and said that recent broader course offerings to include other cultures were major steps forward. Lawrence was the recipient of many accolades, including a MacArthur Fellowship "genius" grant in 1983. Also, he was named a Guggenheim Fellow and served as president of the Organization of American Historians.

Native Languages

The Karuk Indian tribe had no reason to accept **William Bright**. Over a span of more than one hundred years they had been taken advantage of by Europeans and their settlers. Barely 21, William was taken into the Karuk culture by the tribe's grandmothers and named "little word asker". He would become an authority on the native languages and cultures of California while spending more than fifty years inventorying the vanishing tongues of the United States and the globe. He saw language as being inseparable from its cultural context, which could include songs, poetry, stories and everyday conversation. Dragging along large recording devices, William would go into traditional communities around the world, sit down with the native speakers and get them to talk. In recognition of his work to document and preserve their language, the Karuk made him an honorary member of the tribe, the first outsider to receive such a tribute.

The New Look of the Incas

Their South American empire lasted for nearly 135 years in an area that now includes six countries. Once regarded as a civilization of barbaric splendor, **John Murra**'s extensive research into the colonial archives of Spain created a radically new image of the Incas. It was a distinctive people who had developed independent of European or Asian influence. A strong economic system, which John referred to as 'the vertical archipelago', was based on an intricate and often ceremonial exchange of produce as gifts among tribal kinfolk. They would hike from the edges of the rain forest to meet those living at the height of the Andes to insure each other's survival by trading crops for scarce goods. This social system was documented by John with his search through the archives as well as court documents in which the words of the Incas were recorded.

Cultural Anthropologist

Considered a founder of symbolic anthropology, **Clifford Geertz** had an impact on other social sciences and distinguished himself with a literary flair. His field was being challenged to explain what was going on in the non-western world and he responded by focusing on interpreting the symbols he believed gave meaning and order to other people's lives. Drawing on history, psychology and philosophy he analyzed and decoded the meanings of rituals, art, belief systems, institutions and other symbols. Clifford searched for the meaning of cultures and argued that no one could find a common link among all cultures in the world.

Mr. Calculus

It was originally written for college undergraduates in 1951, but **George Thomas**' calculus textbook took on a life of its own. Now in its 11th edition and referred to "Thomas' Calculus", it has become a text in high schools where it is assigned in advanced courses. Covering the branch of math that deals with quantities and limits, areas, and volumes of spaces, his book has introduced countless students to the challenges of functions, derivatives and integrals. It was said of George that he presented calculus in a way that was closer to real math and gave a strong sense of the subject that had not been presented in any earlier books.

Studied US Culture

He once wrote "those who only know one country, know no country". **Seymour Martin Lipset** was one of the most influential social scientists of the last half-century. He first gained attention when he explained the connection between economic development and democracy. Seymour also investigated the nature of political extremism, how the core American values of equality and achievement keep class conflict in check and what other countries can teach the United States. His varied interests in the peculiarities of the US political culture made him a person of interest to journalists, policymakers and academics. Reporters would seek him out to explain such varied issues as a major change in politics and why jokes about gay people were frowned upon.

Public Financing

Called the father of modern public financing, **Richard Musgrave** took twenty years to conceive, write and publish the 1959 book, "The Theory of Public Finance", an analysis of how governments allocate resources to social needs. To this day it is still a work that stands unchallenged and whenever there is a question on the subject, the route to take is through Richard's book. Before his research, most economists focused on the understanding of prices, supply and demand as they interacted with other market forces. Governments played a secondary role, stepping in to fill gaps when the markets failed. Richard felt that the government should play an important role and developed a theory of how choices are made and how governments can perform more efficiently.

The Soliton

Back in 1830's England, a scientist observed a canal boat that suddenly stopped, creating a single wave that sped down the canal while passing through other waves in its path. 130 years would pass before **Martin Kruskal** and a partner would view a similar wave while it transported energy through an atomic crystal. They called it a soliton because of its solitary nature and developed the math to support it. The soliton makes it possible to send multiple signals through fiber optic cables without interference. Martin's work was not confined to this one area. He worked on a classified project that developed a process for controlled nuclear fusion and created a system to describe black holes in space. On the lighter side, he developed a card trick where he used probability to find a reliable way of identifying a playing card picked at random from a given deck. The result would baffle audiences and the trick was adopted by many entertainers who gave it the name the "Kruskal Count".

Highlights

His contributions to science were varied, but **Jack Myers** was best known as the science editor of Highlights for Children magazine. Launched by his parents 60 years ago, Highlights is an educational publication that teaches children in an informal and fun way. Jack would answer more than 400 letters a year from young readers who asked him everything from why human skin wrinkles in water to why dogs walk in circles before they lay down. He also wrote children's books that taught the scientific process with titles like "Can Birds Get Lost" and "What Makes Popcorn Pop?" Jack's talents reached beyond his appeal to the younger set. He won a Founders Award in 1998 for his work on the potential of using algae as food that could be grown on space vehicles.

Helping the Autistic

In the late 1950's, **Sybil Elgar** visited a hospital in England for supposed 'severely emotionally disturbed children'. So-called 'psychotic' children were seen as having a disorder that had been caused by the mother. Parents were told to "put the child away" as the best thing for the family. When Sybil visited the same hospital a few years later she found that nothing had changed. She decided to set up her own school, which, at first, was in the basement of her house. Sybil became the country's first autism-specific teacher and laid the foundations for what is now the accepted program to teach autistic children. In addition, she also established the first residential community for adults with the disorder.

Scholar of Politics

Nelson Polsby was absorbed by the American political process. He wrote or edited 15 books and scores of articles on the subject and was known for his studies of Congress, the presidency, political parties, policymaking and the media. When he entered the world of political science, there was a very traditional historical approach where procedure was studied, but not an investigation into the reasons why Congress acted. Nelson was one of the first to question the behavior of Congress and find out why they did the things they do. Among the subjects he analyzed was how electoral rule changes in the two major parties changed the political landscape.

Televised Ground Rounds

It was the name of a live program broadcast on closed circuit to more than 60 hospitals in Pennsylvania and the Ohio Valley. It presented unusual cases and advances in treatments and connected rural and suburban doctors with specialists at the University of Pittsburgh where **Campbell Moses, Jr.** produced this innovative show in the 1950's and 60's that presented educational television programs to doctors. His on-air expertise was reinforced by his own research. He conducted studies in arteriosclerosis, liver function and nuclear medicine. Later on in his career, Campbell became medical director of the American Heart Association at a time when growing evidence of smoking's harmful effects led to a national ban against cigarette advertising on radio and television.

Family Therapy

Ivan Boszormenyi-Nagy began to look beyond individual psychology in the 1950's and 60's to understand and treat severe mental disorders, especially schizophrenia. He had noticed that destructive patterns of family behavior often went across several generations. He brought patient's grandparents and children into therapy sessions as well as parents and siblings. Ivan found that by working to balance loyalty and obligation among the family, it would help soothe their symptoms and, sometimes, cure them. His work became the foundation for six books and 80 articles on the topic, many of which reached wide translation around the world.

Black People in History

He went back over 3,000 years to trace the lives of black people in the ancient world. **Frank Snowden** documented Greek and Roman encounters with black Africans through many centuries, saying that racial prejudice, as it's viewed today, was largely unknown in ancient times. He went through Greek, Roman, Egyptian, Assyrian, Hebrew and early Christian books and visited museums around the world to examine the depictions of blacks in ancient art. Blacks were revered in those times as charioteers, fighters and actors. Because Romans and Greeks first encountered blacks as soldiers, and not as slaves, they did not see them as inferior. Frank was given a National Humanities Medal in 2003, a top government honor for scholars, writers, actors and artists.

Indiana Jones of Beer

That was the reputation **Alan Eames** earned from his world travels to document the history and origins of beer. He would crawl into Egyptian tombs to read hieroglyphics about beer and boated down the Amazon in search of a mysterious long lost black brew. Alan called himself a beer anthropologist; it was a role that allowed him to discuss any range of topics regarding beer. He traveled to 44 countries and authored seven books on the topic of liquid gold. He was the founding director of the American Museum of Brewing History and Fine Arts in Fort Mitchell, Kentucky which was known for its festive "beer camps".

Sex Education

As early as 1960, during a time when sex was rarely discussed in an open forum in America, **Harold Lief** began organizing the Center for the Study of Sex Education in Medicine at the University of Pennsylvania where he was a professor of psychiatry. It was his goal to make sex education and the treatment of sexual disorders more scientific. At the time, only three other medical schools had separate programs in sexology. Harold was a critic of medical education and frequently made public statements on human sexuality as well as the relationship between psychiatry and the rest of the medical community. He wanted schools to adopt a more serious and scientific approach to teaching medical students about sexuality and development.

Identified Black Landmarks

For nearly twenty years, **Robert DeForrest** and his brother located landmarks throughout the United States that reflected African American history and culture. Working with several federal agencies, they conducted studies that led to more than 60 cites in 22 states and the District of Columbia that were designated as national historic landmarks. In 1970 they established an institute for historic preservation and bought an old mansion in Washington, DC and filled it with photographs, maps, blueprints and other documents that helped them to preserve historic sites and study urban and rural preservation plans and neighborhood development.

Child Development

The New York Longitudinal Study was the unwieldy name for groundbreaking research into human development that began in 1956 and was led by **Stella Chess** and her husband, It followed 133 children from infancy through adulthood and tried to observe patterns of behavior over that period of time. They looked at nine difference facets of behavior and found that most people fell into three broad areas. "Easy", "difficult" or "slow to warm up" described the aspects of a person's temperament and became critically important when matched with a parent's personality, especially the mother's. Their theory suggested that the differences between the mother's personality and her child's could result in behavior or anxiety problems on the part of the child.

Origins of Humans

The earliest work on the study of where humans came from centered more on a "stones and bones" approach by digging up remains and putting a time stamp on them. **Clark Howell** was credited with transforming the work into a broader arena that drew on biology, ecology, geology and primatology. He had led, or participated in, fossil-hunting excavations around the world and Clark's research was not confined by geography nor restricted by academic guidelines. On one excavation, his findings appeared to have extended the trail of human ancestors back nearly six million years, almost twice as early as the prior earliest recognized human ancestor, known commonly as Lucy. As a founder and trustee of the Leakey Foundation, Clark had a wide influence on the field by steering research grants to young scientists working in new areas of scholarship. He had also provided financial backing at a crucial stage in Jane Goodall's work with chimpanzees.

Hyperreality

The French critic **Jean Baudrillard** was the author of more than 50 books and his interests ranged across a wide variety of subject matter. His comments would often spark controversy as his analysis of modern life was too original to fit any one category. One of best known theories centered on his view that the world we live in revolves around simulated feelings and experiences that have replaced the real thing. The 'hyperreality' of mass produced images, from advertising and the media, has drained everything of its authenticity and meaning. Based on this, he encouraged people to give up their search for reality. As an example, the way Jean saw it, Disneyland is presented as imaginary in order to make people believe that the rest is real.

Tracked the Progress of College Enrollment

There was a time when going to college was reserved only for the sons and daughters of the wealthiest households in society. **Martin Trow** monitored the transition of a college education from an elite privilege to a mass product through his 150 articles and 11 books that included the comparative study of educational systems, the issues of learning and teaching as well as the status and academic freedom of university professors. Martin found that once the enrollment numbers began to increase significantly, colleges started to resemble elementary and secondary schools. His best-known paper was issued in 1973 and said that the movement toward universal higher education had made enrollment in college more of a necessity and their presence was sometimes viewed as involuntary.

Greek Database

There had been attempts to gather Greek literature for centuries, but every effort would always fail because it was just too monumental of a task. **Theodore Brunner** launched a project in 1972 to collect all of the Greek texts that have survived since antiquity and digitize them. Included were the first recorded manuscripts of the poet Homer; the comedies and tragedies of Sophocles, Euripides and Aeschylus as well as the histories of Thucydides—everything written in Greek through the sixth century. Today, digitizing is commonplace, but Theodore's project, at the time, was extraordinary. The digital library currently has grown to include nearly all-Greek texts through the 15th century, encompassing nearly 4,000 authors, 12,000 works and 95 million words. It has allowed scholars from around the world to examine ancient texts without having to travel great distances to the colleges, libraries and museums that own each manuscript.

Rapid Diagnosis Strategy

Therapist **Paul Watzlawick** was instrumental in helping to develop a theory known as brief therapy in which behavior or psychological problems were treated in less than 10 sessions. In dealing with marriage problems, family violence and sexual issues, Paul and his colleagues proposed that a patient's attempts to cope actually would aggravate matters. The larger issues became the focus of treatment in order to steer people away from their own ineffective attempts to make themselves feel better. The success rate for this rapid diagnosis approach came in around 75 percent.

Noted Mathematician

A question about 'set theory' was considered to be a problem of major importance for the math world in the 20th century. It involved establishing the sizes of infinite sets of real numbers. **Paul Cohen** had a feeling that the problem was perceived as being hopeless because there was no new method to construct a model for set theory. He ultimately concluded that it could not be solved under the existing framework. In the end, he was celebrated for determining that it couldn't be proved. A primary technique that Paul developed is known as 'forcing' and used to build math models to test a given hypothesis to determine if it is true or not. For disproving set theory, he was awarded the Fields Medal for outstanding achievement, a prize considered to be the math world's equivalent of the Nobel Prize.

Helping Young Readers

The conventional wisdom in the 1960's was not to intervene too early with a child's reading development with the thought that, if they started out slowly, they would be able to catch on by the second or third grade. New Zealander **Marie Clay** observed 100 first-graders for an entire academic year and created a booklet with simple words and pictures for the children to help them begin to form their reading skills. She developed a reading program in the 1970's that was designed to produce results quickly by featuring one-on-one, half-hour sessions each school day for 12 to 20 weeks. The success rate was reported at 80%. Marie exported her program to other countries and introduced programs in English, French and Danish. More than 1.6 million children in the United States have taken advantage of the program in the last twenty years.

Naming Rights

The question arose for him right at birth on why his parents gave him a female sounding name. They liked his sister Elsie's name so his parents took the quick route, slapped a 'K' in front and he had a name. **Kelsie Harder** could identify with the Johnny Cash song, "A Boy Named Sue". He became a leading expert on the origin of names and places and wrote more than 1,000 articles, books, reviews and poems about the starting point for everything that carries a name. He advised Random House Dictionary and headed up the committee of the American Dialect Society. In 1990, he gave the keynote address at the Library of Congress on the 100th anniversary of the US Board on Geographic Names.

Culinary Historian

Karen Hess always believed that history was written in our daily lives. Although not a trained historian, she focused on the importance of primary sources and called on historians to apply the same methods of study as they would use in any other field of history. Karen brought an academic rigor to the study of recipes, cooking techniques and ordinary American kitchen practices. In her first book "The Taste of America", written with her husband in 1977, she sounded the alarm for healthier eating and was critical of the prepackaged "junk food" that had become quite common in the American diet. Karen updated cookbooks, replaced old terms with more familiar current wording, changed around uncommon recipe ingredients and wrote introductions to cookbooks that added a historical context.

Race Relations in a New Light

His 1969 book, "White Over Black", changed forever the understanding of the roots of racism in the United States. **Winthrop Jordan**'s work was important to the discussion of racial attitudes because he explained how perceptions of slavery evolved over time and were not the result of first impressions. He noted that the Englishman's first contact with black Africans, in the early 1600's, was not to see them as slaves, but as another type of person. In the centuries ahead, economic interests, religion, national identity, and differences in skin color brought about the eventual stereotyping that became commonplace and identified the African American race primarily as slaves first. "White Over Black" was a winner of the National Book Award.

Anthropologist with Diverse Interests

Her influence ranged far beyond the traditional areas of her field to examine subjects as wide ranging as kosher diets, consumer behavior, environmentalism and humor as she described how humans work together to find shared meaning. **Mary Douglas** saw little difference between modern and primitive societies. She believed that environmentalists' complaints reflected an antipathy toward the dominant social structure. Mary also contended that buying consumer goods is a method for people to create meaning in their lives and felt that humor served to upset controlled situations. She was made a dame commander of the British Empire and her book, Purity and Danger, was listed by the Sunday London Times as among the 100 most influential books of nonfiction since 1945.

Business Historian

Fortune Magazine recently said that if someone wanted a long-term perspective on the Fortune 500 there was only one person to ask. It was **Alfred Chandler** who the magazine called "America's pre-eminent business historian". Before Alfred, the majority of business history was written as a morality play that portrayed business leaders as heroes or demons. He redirected the field to an objective analysis and argued that the emergence of professional management stimulated the beginnings of modern capitalism. Unlike entrepreneurs, a manager did not need to have a stake in the company in order to lead it. He concluded that the American industrial revolution did not start in the mills of New England, but in the large coalfields of Pennsylvania in the 1830's and '40's. This power source replaced water, wood and charcoal and advanced the manufacture of iron and metal products. Alfred won the Pulitzer Prize for History in 1977 for his book "The Visible Hand".

Researched the Impact of TV Violence

Some people actually suggested that his work was part of a communist conspiracy. Beginning in 1960, **Leonard Eron** began pioneering studies of youth violence that led to the conclusion that television had a significant role in prompting destructive behavior later in life. 8-year-old children, and their parents, were interviewed with their behavior evaluated, and a database created, to follow the children into adulthood. The study still continues to this day. Leonard found that violent parents were an important factor in the development of overly aggressive children and a long-term association between early exposure to violence and aggression later in life held true for both sexes. The overall message of the study was clear: the more violence children watched on television, the more aggressive they became in school.

Authority on France

He was born in Romania and educated in America, but was renowned for his histories of France. **Eugen Weber** published more than a dozen distinguished books on France that have been translated into several languages and are considered classics by the French. As a professor at UCLA, hundreds of thousands of students, over a 40-year period, got their first taste of modern European history from his best selling textbooks. His well-received 52-part lecture series, "The Western Tradition", made for public television in 1989 became the basis of a video instructional series with companion books that are still in use. Eugen's focus was on the many facets of everyday life—how people lived, what food they ate and the houses they lived in. He was decorated by France in 1977 for his contributions to French culture.

Educarer

Thirty years ago, it was generally felt that parents and other adult caregivers should set the course for what, and when, babies learn. **Magda Gerber** founded an organization in 1978 that focused on the importance of babies and following their cues as the best way to foster their growth. Her approach took into account that a baby's response should be looked at closely to help them with their self-development. The field of infant education gradually began to adopt Magda's theories. She was recognized internationally for her work and authored several books on child rearing.

Mr. Wizard

He liked to talk to children as if they were adults and aroused their curiosity in an informal manner that turned obscure science concepts into fun. **Don Herbert** hosted the "Watch Mr. Wizard" television show for 14 years and gained the attention of millions of kids who wanted to explore the mysteries of science. The program was focused on youngsters between the ages of 8 and 13. A few years after it started in 1951, more than 100,000 children were enrolled in 5,000 Mr. Wizard Science clubs. Don had no advanced degree in science and used household items in his TV lab while being assisted by boys and girls. During the 1960's and 70's, half of the doctoral applicants at Rockefeller University cited Mr. Wizard as the reason they first became interested in science. The show won a Peabody Award in 1953 for young people's programming.

Computer Science

He never attained an advanced degree and was one of the very few professors at highly regarded Caltech that did not have one. **John Todd** was a trendsetter in the development of number analysis for computers, played a key role in creating some of the first computers and the courses he taught at Caltech led to the advancement of scientific computing. His greatest contribution came in saving the Mathematical Research Institute in Germany at the end of World War II when he took over a building housing a group of prisoners of war who were performing math calculations for the

Germans. John's actions prevented a group of Moroccan soldiers from destroying the institute and its work.

Prime Number Theorem

It describes the distribution of prime numbers in the universe of whole numbers. Prime numbers are those that can be evenly divided only by themselves and by one—such as three, seven and eleven. The prime number theorem had been formulated in the 18th century and proved one hundred years later. **Atle Selberg** made his mark in 1949 when his theoretical work on the properties of numbers was recognized by the Fields Medal, often referred to as the Nobel Prize of mathematics and awarded to promising mathematicians under the age of 40. He also developed the Selberg trace formula that relates the geometry of certain types of surfaces to the frequencies at which they can vibrate; something like the way the shape of a drum determines the sound it makes.

Historian of Quilts

The story of quilt making was naturally pieced together from castoff patches of information. When she was inducted into the Quilters Hall of Fame in 1983, it was said that **Cuesta Benberry**'s research was so fundamental that she would be quoted in the text, or her name would appear, in every quilt book published. Her collection included an array of patterns, from those typical in the time of Colonial America, to the variety of fabrics pieced together in blocks that became available as the textile industry flourished in the 1800's. Cuesta was particularly interested in the quilts made by black quilt makers and surveyed their work from the days when slave women stitched bedcovers all the way through to modern day creations.

ENGINEERING

Modern Tract Homes

The San Fernando Valley in California was ripe for a housing boom after World War II. Formerly a large farming area, it was quickly being transformed into a sprawling bedroom community by war veterans and others who were moving West for the lure of goods jobs, low cost housing and a sunny climate. Along with his partner, **Dan Saxon Palmer** designed modernist tract homes that would become the building blocks for Southern California's construction boom in the 1950's. They took housing that was affordable and created good, decent contemporary homes. In all, more than 20,000 homes were designed by Dan and his partner and were built by developers not only in California, but also in Arizona, Nevada, Texas and Florida.

Disney Parks

'Cool' was his middle name. **Don Edgren** never met an engineering challenge he couldn't handle. He helped get Disneyland ready for its opening in 1954 and was later hired by Walt Disney to work directly for the company when the Matterhorn attraction needed to be built. Many engineers said it was impossible to put toboggans, a sky ride and waterfalls all inside the Matterhorn, but Don got it done. He put together one of Disney's exhibits at the 1964 World's Fair by building vehicles on a fixed track which moved people through the building. The setup became a fixture for many future Disney rides. He also was instrumental in putting together the New Orleans Square, Pirates of the Caribbean and Space Mountain attractions. Don was named a Disney Legend in 2006, an honor given to people who have had a lasting effect on the Walt Disney Company.

ENVIRONMENT

Flood Plains

After closely studying the several times that the Mississippi River severely flooded in the first half of the 20th century, **Gilbert White** challenged the then-widely held view that natural hazards were best controlled by engineers and construction. At the time, his comments were considered radical, but eventually would gain widespread acceptance. Gilbert became known as the father of flood plain management for his range of alternatives that included flood proofing buildings, emergency evacuation procedures and dams and upstream watershed treatment. He would say that floods were acts of God, but flood losses are largely the acts of people. Gilbert helped to forge international cooperation on water systems in the Middle East, Southeast Asia and Africa as well as assisting in preventing the spread of deserts and warning about the impact of human behavior on the global climate. He was awarded the National Medal of Science in 2000.

Climate Change

The Fairbridge curve is a record of sea level changes over the past 10,000 years. Developed by **Rhodes Fairbridge**, the curve consists of a graph that shows periodic dips and spikes in sea levels against a larger trend of rising ocean water. It is considered to be early evidence of a larger trend in global climate change resulting in the melting of glaciers and continental ice sheets. Rhodes looked at high-water marks recorded in fossilized dunes and reefs and later made additional observations of climate fluctuations. He was also well recognized in his field for editing a series of encyclopedias on the earth sciences including oceanography, geochemistry, atmospheric conditions and regional geology. As a widely traveled field geologist,

Rhodes wrote articles for the series, published in 1966, which is still in use today as a key reference source.

Smog Particles

After joining UCLA in 1983, **Sheldon Friedlander** founded the school's laboratory to monitor air quality. Within a few years he was searching for an easier and cheaper way to trap smokestack emissions as Sheldon wanted to control toxic wastes before they're produced and not wait to deal with them after they've already entered the environment. He was able to devise a method to analyze existing data that measured the chemical makeup of smog particles and unraveled what was contributing to air pollution at any given time. It was a breakthrough that led to a greater understanding and regulation of the problem.

Monkey World

With a passion for animals, **Jim Cronin** envisioned building his own wild-life park. In 1987 he bought an old pig farm and built fenced-in enclosures. Having heard about baby chimps being used as photographer's props in Spain, Jim worked with local animal activists there and brought back 35 chimpanzees with him. They were the beginning of Monkey World, a 62-acre park that now draws about 500,000 a year. Featured on the cable show "Monkey Business", it appears about 14 times a year in nearly 200 countries on the Animal Planet channel. Monkey World is home to 165 animals, including 59 chimps, 13 orangutans and 18 gibbons as well as woolly monkeys, marmosets, lemurs and capuchin monkeys.

Scarcity of Fish

It was said that he brought a childlike glee to the collection and analysis of fishing records and he had a unique ability to look at complex global changes and pick out trends that others had missed. **Ransom Myers** spent years poring over five decades of Japanese log books and determined that 90% of the world's sharks, tuna, swordfish, cod and other large predatory fish had been stripped from the seas by industrialized fishing since the 1950's. Ransom made it known that humans have always been very good at killing large land-based animals in the past and, without oversight, that same could happen in the oceans. A report released in 2003 by Ransom and his team said that fishing pressure had become so great that few fish were able to live long enough to reach full size or reproduce. In 2005, Fortune magazine named him one of the top 10 people in the world to watch.

Bird Talk

Over forty years ago, **Dwight Chamberlain** did early research on common crows, recording them in order to be able to classify them and understand the function of their calls. He found 11 distinct calls, among them the signals for crows to gather together, to fly away, the call of hunger and even the call of impending death. Dwight found that the birds make a squalling call as an emergency signal for help that is intended to summon other crows quickly. He later became a public educator, speaking about birds and the need for conservation. He tamed and raised a raven and appeared with it at schools and nature centers to enlighten the public about the complexities of birds.

Canoeing in the Pacific

The question of how more than 1,000 islands of Polynesia were settled has long perplexed scientists. The question had always been whether fisherman had washed up on the islands by accident or accomplished seamen purposely found their way to the massive chain that covers more than 10 million square miles of the Pacific Ocean. In 1976, **Kawika Kapahulehua** became the first captain in nearly 600 years to set sail from Hawaii to Tahiti in a canoe. The vessel was a 62-foot-long, two-mast that was believed to closely resemble an ancient oceangoing canoe. Using only the sky and sea to navigate, Kawika commanded the double-hulled boat on a journey of 2,250 miles and 34 days. Although it could not prove that ancient explorers discovered the islands in this manner, the trip demonstrated that long-distance navigation with a specific destination is possible.

Altruistic Plant Grower

Zonal gardening is based on the idea that certain plants can only grow in particular climates. **Polly Hill** put that notion to rest through 40 years of planting seeds she had gathered from around the world and proved that trees and shrubs that thrive in warm environs can also survive in the cold winter. As an amateur scientist, botanist and plant geneticist, Polly created what she called her "playpen", a planting area the length of a football field that was surrounded by a ten foot high fence. She grew more than 1,700 varieties of plants and introduced over 100 species. Polly was known in the field for her detailed record keeping as she traced the viability of every seed she planted. She never sold her seeds, but gave them away to other plant growers around the globe. Her property in Massachusetts has been open, free of charge, for decades.

The Environmental Cause

Right at the forefront, **Alexander King** warned of the dangers to the environment from extensive industrial development and was among a group who commissioned the 1972 Limits to Growth report that triggered the first wave of international concern about the environment. The book still remains one of the world's best sellers on the environment having sold 12 million copies in 37 languages. It struck a raw nerve and resulted, a few months after publication, in the establishment of an environmental program within the United Nations in which Alexander had a key role in expanding its reach. He became one of the founders of the international think-tank, the Club of Rome, which was referred to as "the conscience of the world".

Walked to the North Pole

At the age of 12 he walked across a river that had ice barely thick enough to support him. With that experience, **Wally Herbert** adopted a fascination with travel on ice. In the Arctic Ocean, the constantly shifting frozen cover can produce unpredictable patterns of thick ice or turn to mush and not be able to hold up even one dog. He set out in February 1968 from

Alaska facing temperatures of 30 below Celsius and spent the next sixteen months being guided at night by the lights of the Aurora Borealis as he and his team made their way to Norway, 1,500 miles away. After thorough research years later, it was revealed that Wally and his team were the first to walk to the North Pole and not Robert Peary, who had been credited for the trek nearly 80 years earlier.

Rare Fruit

It was on a sailing trip to Tahiti that **Bill Whitman** was captivated by the island's unique species and variety of rare fruit. As a self-taught horticulturalist, he became renowned for collecting rare tropical fruits from around the world and popularized them in the United States. Bill was the only person to have brought an Asian mangosteen tree to the US and cultivated it to prosper although it was known to be notoriously finicky and cold sensitive. He also created attention for miracle fruit, a berry that tricks the palate into thinking that sour tastes sweet. Bill's interests were wide and varied. In addition to fruit, he and his brothers helped to popularize surfing in Florida and he was inducted into the East Coast Surfing Hall of Fame.

Preserved the Land

The Nature Conservancy was started in 1951 as a nonprofit that has protected 15 million acres of land in the United States and 29 other countries. **Richard Goodwin** was a founder of the organization and twice served as its president. He helped to negotiate the preservation of 3,000 acres of forest along the coast of Northern California, one of the largest land-trust deals in the Conservancy's history. In an east coast preserve they established, more than 100 types of trees, shrubs and vines grow as well as more than 400 varieties of flowering plants. Membership has grown from 2,500 in the mid-1950's to nearly 1 million today.

Beekeeper

It was certainly a different type of wedding present. **Eva Crane**'s interest in bees began when she received a beehive on the day she was married. She would say that she really wasn't interested in the bees as much as how they worked together, how different people keep bees and why they keep them. Founding the Bee Research Association in 1949, Eva was its director for 35 years. She had earned a doctorate in physics, but spent her career working in more than 60 countries, traveling by canoe or dogsled to document the human use of bees from prehistoric times to the present. Among her many interesting findings: Babylonians used honey to preserve corpses; bees were used as military weapons by the Viet Cong and beekeepers in Pakistan were using the same type of hive that was used in ancient Greece.

The Real Indiana Jones

His flair for self-promotion drew on his tales of finding ancient ruins in Peru and adventurous perils in the jungle. **Gene Savoy** was labeled by People magazine as the real life version of the Harrison Ford character in the Raiders of the Lost Ark movies. He had sought out the Fountain of Youth, the Treasure of El Dorado, proof that Solomon's gold had come from South America and had a quest to find the answers in life. He was credited with finding four of Peru's most important sites, including Vilcabamba, the last refuge of the Incas from Spanish conquistadors. Over a forty-year period, Gene discovered more than 40 stone cities of a mysterious pre-Inca civilization. It was thought that the existence of those cities was a myth until he opened up a new area of jungle archaeology that had not existed.

Snow Leopards

The first time she set eyes on two snow leopards at a zoo in Seattle, **Helen Freeman** was captivated by what she saw. Spending hours at a time at the Woodland Park Zoo, she observed their behavior and became an expert at interpreting their manner. In 1981 she founded the Snow Leopard Trust to preserve them in their endangered habitat in Central Asia. She traveled throughout the United States, Europe and Asia to pursue stronger protection for wild leopards. Helen was ahead of her time in helping people living in areas where the snow leopards are common to improve their standard of living in exchange for assistance in helping the animals to thrive in their habitat.

MEDICINE

Breast Cancer Screening

In the 1980's there was a divided opinion about the risks and effectiveness of mammograms for young women who showed no signs of breast cancer. **Arthur Holleb** introduced guidelines that called for a more vigorous national effort at early detection for women under 50. As chief medical officer of the American Cancer Society and a breast cancer specialist, he found that there were substantial benefits in breast X-rays every two to three years for women between 40 to 49. Today, mammograms are recommended for any woman over the age of 40. Arthur also spoke out about cancer risks from smoking and the manipulation of young women by cigarette manufacturers. In the 60's and 70's he promoted the Pap test to detect cervical cancer in women.

Researched Heart Attacks and Strokes

Applying the principles of engineering to problems in medicine and biology is as old as science itself. **John Lever** made the focus of his career the study of heart arteries and tracing the conditions that underlie the development of atherosclerosis. He generated a series of papers that substantially advanced the understanding of the processes that are responsible for the accumulation of fatty material in vessel walls and the impact of smoking, hypertension and blood flow. In his collaborations with physicists, engineers and medical doctors, John used novel and emerging techniques, such as fluorescent and infrared imaging, to study the composition of plaque in artery walls.

Polio Vaccine

In the summer of 1952 there were over 57,000 new cases of polio reported with some victims becoming paralyzed or dying as a result. Within two years, Jonas Salk had developed an effective vaccine that needed to be tested on children. Many health departments turned a cold shoulder to the experiment due to concerns that the trial could fail. Popular radio broadcaster Walter Winchell had taken to the airwaves opposing the test and scared off potential volunteers. **Richard Mulvaney** was a family doctor in McLean, Virginia who accepted the challenge and became the first physician to conduct a field test of the experimental vaccine when he inoculated a six-year-old boy. By 1955 the number of polio cases had dropped to slightly over 29,000. When the oral version of the vaccine was introduced seven years later, polio became a disease of the past.

Bone Marrow Transplants

When bone marrow transplants were first introduced in the treatment of leukemia, the procedure could only be performed when the patient had a close family member who had a matching marrow. Children with no siblings had no chance of surviving. **Anthony Oakhill** was able to pioneer techniques in Britain that saved the lives of hundreds of children who otherwise would have died. He put his department at Bristol Children's Hospital at the forefront of the two most important advances for the disease in over twenty years. One improvement was widening the use of potential donors beyond immediate family members. The other change was the refinement of techniques to detect the presence of residual leukemia that can still be present after treatment, but can't be found by conventional methods. The results proved to be as good as, if not better than, sibling transplants.

Specialized in Dementia

While director of a study that was examining the effects of aging on memory, **Leonard Berg** began to assemble the elements of what became the Clinical Dementia Rating Scale, a measurement that is now widely used in

Alzheimer's research. Leonard and his team combined tests of memory and language with an assessment of the patient's ability to interact in the community. The patient was asked questions about their daily activities, hobbies and everyday tasks such as balancing a checkbook. Each response would result in a number score, with 0 showing no symptoms and .5 indicating the possibility of the onset of dementia while 3.0 would be interpreted as severely suffering from the disease. The rating scale has led to a more precise measurement of a patient's condition and has provided an important benchmark for clinicians to determine whether dementia has advanced.

Family Therapy

The approach he used ran counter to the method a traditionalist would use. **Jay Haley** promoted brief therapies that focused on solving concrete and immediate problems rather than looking into the past to try to identify root causes. He advocated hypnosis and extended social involvement for patients to cure emotional problems more rapidly. Jay was a trainer and teacher of therapists and not a psychologist. He encouraged techniques that were considered unconventional like giving patients homework and tasks outside of the consulting session that would lead to a more lasting and spontaneous resolution of problems.

Fight Against Malaria

Sent out with the instructions "come back when you have something to tell me", **Ian McGregor** traveled through the most remote villages of Africa in search of determining the relationship between nutrition and disease caused by parasites. His early contributions to malaria research were by the simple processes of looking at blood smears with a microscope and sitting under the shade of a mango tree examining thousands of patient's livers and spleens. His surveys established a wealth of information that is still in use today. Ian was able to demonstrate how parasitic diseases can start a downward cycle where infections reduce the body's nutrients and, in turn, reduces a person's resistance that leads to a further invasion of parasites. His findings that an immunity could be created through repeated exposure to malaria helped significantly in the understanding of acquired immunity.

The Growth of Children

Today, the long-term study of people from birth to adulthood is common-place. Pediatrician **Neville Butler** was an innovator in the field when he first began a study that tracked the births of all 17,000 babies in one week in March 1958 in England. He would later set up the second of Britain's three internationally recognized birth studies and inspired a generation of researchers to study the consequences of early childhood experience and the factors that reinforce positive and negative development in people's lives. Subjects as diverse as the effects of smoking in pregnancy and the origins of adults' basic-skills difficulties have been enhanced by Neville's work.

A Vaccine to Prevent Infections

After the introduction of penicillin and other antibiotics after World War II, most doctors assumed that infections would no longer be a major cause of death and they stopped prescribing a preventative vaccine. **Robert Austrian** was startled to find that, in the 1960's, there were half as many pneumonia deaths in the United States as there were at the turn of the century. Through his work he showed that pneumonia continued to be a killer and two vaccines were licensed for use to reduce the number of deaths. Robert proved their safety and effectiveness by supervising clinical trials among military trainees and gold miners in South Africa because they were at greater risk when they worked in crowded conditions. Throughout his long career, Robert continued to help determine whether additional strains of pneumonia needed to be added to future vaccines by studying samples sent to him by doctors around the world.

Huntington's

She was seen swaggering along a Los Angeles street over forty years ago. The police officer assumed that she was drunk, but instead she was show-ing the telltale signs of Huntington's disease, a rare incurable genetic disorder that had already killed her father and three brothers. **Marvin Wexler** was concerned that the disease would strike their two daughters and set out to do what he could to prevent it from happening. Trained as a lay psychoanalyst, he formed the Hereditary Disease Foundation to gather young scientists from different areas for wide ranging discussions about Huntington's. By 1983 they were able to identify the approximate location of the gene and, ten years later, specifically identified the gene. Many scientists had believed that the progress they made in only a few decades might have taken 100 years. Their efforts also demonstrated the feasibility of mapping the entire array of 30,000 human genes.

The Risk of Smoking

As concerns grew in the 1960's about the health risks of tobacco use, the US Surgeon General asked **Peter VanVechten Hamill** to assemble a ten person advisory committee to investigate the connection between cigarette smoking and cancer. Peter and many of the panel members were smokers at the beginning of the study, but by the end they all had quit. The report that medically defined and confirmed that smoking causes cancer was issued to the public on Saturday, January 11, 1964. The day was chosen to release the data to limit the effect on the stock market and to make sure that the report would receive maximum coverage. A year later, Congress responded by requiring that all cigarette packages include the now well-known health warning: "the surgeon general has determined that cigarette smoking is dangerous to your health."

Medical Marijuana

It had been available for one hundred years and was taken off the market in 1938 following a backlash from the release of the movie "Reefer Madness" which depicted marijuana smokers as social outcasts. He was called a savior by some and a menace by others. Back in the 1960's, **Tod Mikuriya** began to research the therapeutic values of marijuana and compiled a list of more than 200 ailments it was believed to cure—including stuttering, insomnia, premenstrual syndrome, writer's cramp, poor appetite and some side effects of cancer. He was the architect of a California state ballot measure that passed in 1996 and permitted doctors there to recommend marijuana for seriously ill patients. Tod was reported to have approved the drug for nearly 9,000 patients.

Alcoholism in the Navy

Forty years ago, alcoholism and its effects on behavior were considered as violations of Navy policy that was punishable by time in the brig. The reality was that the atmosphere on base and at sea encouraged heavy drinking. **Joseph Zuska** began an underground program at Long Beach Naval Station and treated alcoholism as a medical problem. His treatment was the first in the history of the armed forces and it eventually earned national recognition and became a model for other branches of the military and private industry. By the late 60's, the Pentagon gave Joseph approval for the first official Alcohol Rehabilitation Center. Within three years, 70% of 900 admitted patients showed significant improvement.

Institute of Medicine

Congress created the National Academy of Sciences in the mid-1800's to advise the government and the public in all areas of science. The Academy, in turn, created a medical arm, the Institute of Medicine, in 1970. As its first president, **John Hogness** molded it to be an independent critic of the nation's health care system. He set a goal of identifying health problems and bringing them to the public's attention before they turned into crises. John also became involved in issues surrounding care at the end of life and criticized medicine as encouraging a society that sought a pill to solve every ailment. He promoted rigid standards for the prescription of any drug and studied the long-term effects of drugs for chronic illness. National health insurance was a focus as John said that a university needed to look beyond training health professionals and examine and help solve national health problems.

Forensic Psychiatry

Spearheading the development of new secure services for mentally challenged offenders, **James MacKeith** worked to uphold the rights of people in detention and helped to remedy wrongful convictions. With a colleague, James' research studies and casework were crucial in demonstrating, despite much criticism, the existence of false confessions. He covered how they take place and the potential unreliability of criminal convictions based on unconfirmed accusations. At a time when many courts were still treating psychiatric evidence with near contempt while clinging to outdate concepts of mental capacity, James swept aside that viewpoint not only in England, but around the world.

An Early Fighter Against AIDS

When there had been only 1,450 reported cases of AIDS in 1983, **Edward Brandt** called the disease the Number One priority of the Public Health Service. As the acting surgeon general of the Service, he worked with great difficulty to overcome bureaucratic and political obstacles to allocate more money. He established a government hotline to provide information about the outbreak and appointed prominent researchers to head teams searching for what caused AIDS, how it spread and how it could be treated. Edward was also instrumental in finding a way for the disease control centers to build a maximum-security laboratory that was needed to investigate a growing number of dangerous microbes. A medical doctor by training, he led several medical schools and was president of the University of Maryland at Baltimore.

Heart Failure Treatment

Edmund Sonnenblick was the first to use an electron microscope to image heart muscle under controlled conditions when he correlated measurements of heart muscle structure and the force of its contractions. His work formed the basis for the modern treatment of heart failure that has been able to extend the lives of millions of people. At the time of Edmund's breakthrough in the 1960's, doctors knew that a healthy heart could adjust to pump more blood when less flowed into it, but they did not understand the best way to treat a failing heart that could not make that adjustment. He trained more than 300 cardiologists and researchers and received the Distinguished Scientist Award in 1985. In 2007, the

American Heart Association named him the recipient of one of its highest prizes.

The Nervous System

By the 1940's it became apparent that some diseases might be caused by an inappropriate response on the part of a patient's immune system that would produce antibodies against their own tissues. **John Newsom-Davis** observed that those diseases might be temporarily controlled by the exchange of the patient's blood plasma with normal plasma. His greatest contribution was to identify appropriate treatments in neurological diseases that, like Parkinson's and Alzheimer's, can be chronic and progressive. Laboratory methods were established that aided in the detection of antibodies and ensured that neurologists could make the proper diagnosis and treatment. John helped to define several genetic diseases that involved the junction between the nerve and the muscle, but are not caused by the immune system and require different treatments.

SCIENCE

Used One Science to Understand Another

It was said that **Nelson Leonard** was way ahead of his time. Before it was accepted practice, he collaborated with biochemists and biologists long before an exchange among sciences was the norm. He was one of the first to use chemistry to understand biology. Starting in the 1960's, Nelson and his students made changes to chemicals that affect the growth and development of plants. Several of the chemicals proved to be potent stimulators of plant cell growth and division and are now widely used to start the growth of plants, flowers and trees from tissue culture. In the following decade he began new work to help show where specific chemicals were located within a cell. The studies helped to result in a body of knowledge that makes up much of what is known today on how a cell works. Nelson had been a member of the National Academy of Sciences since 1955.

Radio Astronomer

As one of Britain's leading radio astronomers, **Jim Cohen** devoted his career to understanding the physics behind the evolution and formation of stars and led the search to find a method to protect optical astronomy from light pollution and radio astronomy from interference. By using radio beacons, Jim was able to understand how magnetic fields influence both the birth and aging process of stars. He was also concerned with protecting the radio spectrum so sensitive observations could continue to use large telescopes. Jim participated in negotiations with commercial users who wanted to transmit more power across a greater piece of the spectrum and helped to reach a compromise with an agreement that allowed scientific users to have parts of the spectrum quiet in order to receive very weak signals from distant stars and galaxies.

The Origins of Autism

At first, autism was considered by doctors to be the result of the "refrigerator mother"—a cold, indifferent parent who forced their child to withdraw. When **Bernard Rimland**'s son developed the symptoms of autism, he concluded that the disorder was the result of a fundamental biochemical defect due possibly to defective genes and triggered by the environment. He was among the first to discover that the United States was undergoing an epidemic of autism in which one of every 175 children was affected. His landmark 1964 book "Infantile Autism" broke the barrier for understanding autism's effects. He believed that mercury in vaccines was the primary culprit and led a campaign to have it removed, but it was met with limited success due to some government and medical authorities disagreeing with his conclusion. Bernard founded the Autism Society of America that now has more than 100,000 members and supporters and 200 local chapters.

Father of Modern Gem Research

In the 1950's, a supply of relatively rare yellow diamonds had appeared on the gem market. This led to questions about their authenticity that couldn't be confirmed due to the lack of sophisticated technology available. **G. Robert Crowningshield** introduced the spectroscope that became a powerful tool for jewelers and gemologists to use to evaluate the legitimacy and color of any diamond. He made thousands of significant contributions to the study of gems and laid the foundation of modern gem research. He came up with a diamond grading system that is now the worldwide standard and introduced the familiar phrase to bridegrooms—the need to determine the "cut, color, clarity and carat weight". In 1997, the Gemological Institute of America named its research facility after him. The lab is considered to be one of the best in the world.

Nutrition Expert

His interest was in the benefits of eating dietary fiber, the effects of saturated and unsaturated fats and the role of fat in promoting cancer and heart disease. **David Kritchevsky** was a biochemist who published an early and influential textbook in the late 1950's, "Cholesterol", which explored the workings of the fatty substance found in cells and in the bloodstream and considered a significant factor in coronary problems. David once said that you can eat a Hershey bar if you want to, but don't live on Hershey bars. A prime rib steak is fine as long as you're not eating ten pounds a week. He stressed throughout his career that smoking, lack of exercise, overeating and other poor behaviors were too often discounted and could be at least as harmful to health as poor nutrition.

The Stealth Virus

While conducting experiments with bacteria, **Esther Lederberg** discovered a previously unreported virus that was infecting the bacteria while doing no immediate harm to the host organism. After the virus was transmitted through bacteria and ordinary genetic material it would normally remain dormant or sometimes come awake and destroy the host. With her discovery of the "lambda phage", Esther had identified a key tool for the laboratory study of viruses and genetics. Building on her work, her husband John won the 1958 Nobel Prize for Physiology or Medicine for his discoveries on how bacteria swap genes. In addition, the couple also developed the technique known as replica plating which simplified the procedure to perform the rapid screening of bacteria in order to identify mutations.

Insect Borne Diseases

He braved jungles and deserts and the worst political conditions hoping to save lives. **Andrew Spielman** studied mosquitoes, ticks and other insects to shed light on the diseases that parasites carry to humans. Malaria, the West Nile virus and Lyme disease were his main focus. Andrew was interested in how disturbances in the environment brought about by agriculture encouraged the outbreak of sickness in Africa. His most notable research came in Nantucket Massachusetts in the 1970' when he observed that deer ticks were valuable in understanding the transmission of Lyme disease which was then in the early stages of its diagnosis. Andrew suggested that a reduction in the deer population would lead to a decline in the disease. That strategy is now widely applied to prevent the spread of Lyme, which deer ticks can transmit.

Created New Rice Plant

While working for the International Rice Research Institute in the 1960's, **Henry Beachell** crossed rice plants from Taiwan and Indonesia to produce a new variety of plant that was shorter and sturdier than earlier versions. It was less prone to damage during a harvest and quicker to cultivate. The gain for subsistence farmers was a significantly larger annual yield of rice that often amounted to two to three times the size of other plant yields. For his advancements in agriculture, Henry received the Japan Prize in 1987 and was awarded a World Food Prize nine years later.

Probed Into Cardiovascular Disease

It was known that the combination of smoking and high cholesterol in young men could damage their arteries, but the research of **Robert Wissler** found that the problem could arise much earlier and be more significant than was previously known. In looking at blood vessels in men between 15 and 34 who had died suddenly without evidence of chronic disease, Robert's team of researchers discovered that fatty streaks, which can lead to artery plaque, were present in some cases and smokers were at risk of developing lesions on their artery and aorta. The study supported his belief that heart disease could often be minimized or even prevented by changing a patient's diet and reducing the amount of fat intake.

The Variety of Marine Life

He would jump aboard freighter ships while he was a college undergraduate and stow away as a hobo to experience the life at sea. **John Sieburth** was studying the use of antibiotics to prevent turkey disease when he acquired an interest in investigating claims that penguins had no bacteria in their systems. Traveling to Antarctica, he identified extremely small ocean organisms that appear to be the most abundant on earth. Throughout his career he devised new experimental methods and was part of a generation of ocean scientists who used technology to vastly expand the knowledge of ocean life.

Scholar of the Heavens

His influential textbook for graduate students was written to explain the use of basic physics and understand the sun and the shape of the Milky Way. **Donald Osterbrock** had an interest in clusters of stars and the dust within clouds that emit a telltale glow and are known as gaseous nebulae. He was renowned for discovering the internal processes that revealed how the sun kept its size and demonstrated why the outer portion of the sun is hotter than its surface. He mapped out the star-forming regions of the Milky Way and proved that it is shaped like a spiral. In 1997, Donald was awarded the Gold Medal by the Royal Astronomical Society in England, its highest honor and an award rarely given to an American.

ALD

It is a disease that affects one in every 20,000 males and comes from a genetic disorder that causes a host of terrible problems, including deafness, seizures and difficulty with movement. Once the symptoms appear, children normally die within a few years. **Hugo Moser** was vilified in the movie "Lorenzo's Oil" as an uncaring clinical neurologist who was unaffected by the suffering of his patients, but the reality was he had a reputation as a compassionate and energetic researcher. He identified the abnormalities that were behind the genetic disorder that causes ALD, developed a screening test to diagnose it, tested potential treatments and was working on refining a test for newborns at the time he passed away. Hugo had been working on ALD since 1955 and developed the first blood plasma test to identify the disease. It was an important step because many forms of the disease had been misdiagnosed.

Research Duo

They were partners in life, both as husband and wife and professionally as research scientists in the same lab. Both passed away within four days of each other. **David Perkins** was a pioneer in genetic research that established a fungus as a model organism to be used in experiments. For nearly 60 years he compiled data on more than 1,000 fungus genes while he traveled the world to collect more than 5,000 samples. His efforts applied to human cells and gave scientists the ability to understand how glucose can be converted into energy. Two Nobel Prize-winners used the mold he created to show the relationship between genes and enzymes. **Dorothy Perkins** worked in David's lab for over 30 years while writing 30 papers under another name.

Treating the Eye

George Duncan was at the forefront of groundbreaking research on human eye tissue. For most of his career, he focused on the causes and treatments of cataracts. His work identified the failure to handle calcium as a major cause of this eye affliction. George widened his investigation by studying the control of growth, and development, of the cells of the lens with his laboratory becoming a world center for research. His work identified the factors that were involved in unusual cell growth that complicated the success of cataract surgery. The results of George's efforts are currently being developed to help establish new treatments.

Family Based Therapy

For 30 years **Lyman Wynne** conducted a study in Finland that looked at the interaction of genes and the environment in developing schizophrenia. He eliminated the belief that a child's early family environment, especially the mother, causes the problem. Lyman did determine that stressful social environments could increase the likelihood that genetically vulnerable people will develop schizophrenia. His findings prompted therapists to include family members in helping during treatment, whenever possible, and made clearer how genes influence the progress of this mental disorder.

Whale Man

Many people in Southern California knew **John Heyning** as "Whale Man", a nickname he earned from decades of carting away stranded whales from area beaches. Using a truck that was custom fitted with a whale-sized wench, he could collect as many as 30 marine mammals a year. As a marine biologist with the Natural History Museum of Los Angeles County, he dramatically furthered research on marine mammals. At more than 4,000, John helped to build the museum's collection of marine mammal specimens into the second largest in the world. Only the Smithsonian Institution has more.

Plastic Electricity

Before 1977, plastics were used for Styrofoam cups, nylons and polyester for clothes. By accident, a researcher in Japan mixed 1,000 times too much of a chemical into an experiment. Instead of the intended result it produced a silvery film. **Alan MacDiarmid**, along with the mistaken researcher and a third academic, discovered that plastic could be made electrically conductive. They found a way to convert plastic into metal so that electrons could move freely through it. Unlike metal, plastic is flexible and can be manipulated when needed. As a result of their discovery, the antistatic coating on camera film and the bright displays on cell phones benefited from their work. In 2002, Alan and his colleagues shared the Nobel Prize in Chemistry.

Aerospace Innovator

While working as a research scientist for Union Carbide in the 1950's, **Roger Bacon** experimented with materials that he exposed to high pressure and electricity when he found fibers that were smaller than a tenth of a human hair and were stronger than steel. Later on, Roger made carbon fibers by heating them to 3,000 degrees Celsius. As a result, the fiber conducted little heat and resisted expanding. In the 1960's, the fibers were mixed with other materials to protect the edges, noses and wingtips of planes, missiles and space vehicles. The resulting product was a composite, reinforced with fibers that had strength and was able to repel heat. In 2004, the Franklin Institute in Philadelphia awarded Roger a Benjamin Franklin Medal for Mechanical Engineering.

Fighting Alzheimer's

His fascination with treating this disease began 30 years ago when **Leon Thal** began studies that led him to focus on the role of a chemical element in learning and memory. With that work Leon published some of the first evidence that memory could be improved in Alzheimer's patients by stopping the production of a specific brain enzyme. This finding led to the basis for the first FDA approved drug to stall the progress of the disease. Leon's towering achievement was building the Alzheimer's Disease Cooperative Study in 1991. Since its founding it has attracted $100 million in funding. In 2004, he won the Potamkin Prize, one of neuroscience's highest honors and the most prestigious award in the field of Alzheimer's research.

Kenya's Leading AIDS Researcher

Job Bwayo's groundbreaking studies of the history of the HIV virus in East Africa helped to discover an apparent immunity. In studying a group of sexually active women who were immune from AIDS, Job was able to identify the critical component of their immune system which led to some of the most promising vaccines currently under development. He was instrumental in building a world class clinical research facility and established a team that went on to develop a vaccine that stimulates the generation of the T-cells which help to prevent AIDS.

Jet Lag

The experiment period last more than 35 years as **Charles Ehret** studied the reasons behind the effects of flying long distances in an airplane. Jet lag results from crossing too many time zones too quickly for the body to adjust, resulting in headaches, fatigue and disorientation. Charles found that it could be fixed by adjusting eating and sleep schedules by following a strict system. Using himself as a guinea pig, he persuaded family members and friends to try versions of his diet. He co-authored a book in 1983, "Overcoming Jet Lag", that counted President Ronald Reagan among its many followers. Through the years he continued to fine tune the diet based on thousands of letters he received from travelers.

Skin Expert

Aaron Lerner led a team of researchers at Yale University in 1958 that isolated a hormone from a gland in the brain. Aaron named it 'melatonin' and the compound became instrumental in maintaining the rhythm of sleep and wakefulness and is now used to treat sleeplessness and jet lag. Aaron would also develop a transplant therapy to treat a condition called veiling that leaves light colored patches around the mouth and eyes. By taking a patch of the patient's normal skin, he grew the cells in the lab and then applied them to the damaged areas. The result was a more uniform skin color that greatly improved the patient's appearance.

Multi-Talented Physicist

Starting in the late 1940's, **Albert Baez** helped lay the foundation for the newly developing science of X-ray imaging optics while he was doing graduate work in physics at Stanford University. He created the first X-ray reflection microscope, which could examine living cells. The imaging technique is still used, especially in medicine and in astronomy to take X-ray pictures of galaxies. By the 60's he was making films aimed at improving the teaching of high school physics. The UN's Educational, Scientific and Cultural Organization (UNESCO) named him the first director of its science-teaching division and he was stationed in Paris until 1967. It was there that Albert helped developing nations improve their teaching of math and science. His last name is familiar and, yes, he is the father of folk singer Joan Baez.

Studied Outer Space

His ideas were often at odds with the conventional wisdom and some people thought he was nuts. But in the end **Bohdan Paczynski** revolutionized astronomy by using a special lens that he used as a tool to search for dark matter and new planets. The technique he used works when light from a background star is bent by the pull of a darker object in the foreground.

The result is a magnification of light that yields important information about the fainter object. Einstein's relativity theory was the basis for Bohdan's work. He also made the case that gamma rays could originate outside the Milky Way by observing that they could be anywhere in the universe due to their brightness.

Followed Cosmic Rays

He wanted to understand the source of cosmic rays, the energy they generated and the building blocks that created them. They shower the earth with particles and are known to come from the sun as well as beyond our solar system. **Kenneth Greisen** had developed an influential theory about cosmic rays and how their energy levels change over distance. The premise was that the incoming rays are affected by a background of microwave radiation that still lingers from the effects of the Big Bang. It predicted that rays with higher energy than the limit would be filtered before reaching the Earth. Kenneth conducted a highly innovative experiment in 1971 in which he observed gamma rays at slightly more than 100,000 feet when he and his colleagues attached a radio telescope to an unmanned balloon.

Childhood Cancer

When pediatric oncologist **Jon Pritchard** began his career, the prospect of survival with childhood cancer in England was 30%. Due to his efforts it stands today at 75%. With a small group of doctors, Jon formed a children's cancer study group that worked to establish protocols to treat all types of childhood cancer and promoted a strong program of clinical research. He included parents as honorary members of the treatment team and gave truthful information about side effects and prognoses. By emphasizing the quality of life, Jon strived to alleviate the symptoms and help the children try to maintain, however difficult, a normal degree of life.

The Causes of Diabetes

Holding a variety of academic positions for nearly 50 years at Case Western Reserve University in Cleveland, **Bernard Landau** specialized in researching how the body breaks down and captures carbohydrates like glucose. With other associates, he investigated how tissues process glucose in the liver where it is stored as glycogen. In some types of diabetes, the process of glycogen is disrupted and leads to further complications. By developing methods to follow and measure these metabolic functions, he used radioactive tracers that were placed within bodily tissue. In later years he used isotopes to trace the production of glucose in the liver and followed the body's generation of other simple sugars. With assistance, he also utilized isotopes to examine the biochemical pathway by which glucose is broken down.

The Billings Method

The primary method of natural contraception was the rhythm method which predicted a woman's fertile cycle based on her past menstrual history and the calendar in making a best guess on when the next ovulation period would take place. **John Billings** came up with a technique that relies on a woman's ability to sense changes in the amount and texture of her cervical mucus, a strong indicator that the next cycle is about to begin. It can be used either to prevent conception or to bring it about, with couples abstaining from sex and engaging in it on the woman's most fertile days. First started in Australia in the 1950's, the Billings method is used in more than 100 countries and is the only government sanctioned form of natural childbirth in China.

Boundary Lines

Liquid crystals were discovered in the late 19th century and are now common in computer displays and flat screen TV's. They act in a strange way, flowing like liquid as their molecules line up in the same direction as those in a solid crystal. **Pierre-Gilles de Gennes** did not invent or build liquid crystal displays, L.C.D.'s, but he answered the fundamental questions of how they behave. Working on a wide range of topics, he was able to take solutions from one field of physics and show by analogy how they could solve entirely different problems. He demonstrated that the equations governing superconductors, materials that carry electricity with no resistance, could be applied to liquid crystals even though they have very different physical compositions. Pierre basically studied the boundary lines between between order and disorder in both liquid crystals and polymers. For his work, Pierre was awarded the Nobel Prize in Physics in 1991.

Simulated the Origins of Life

For the first part of the 20th century, scientists had long speculated about how life could have developed on Earth. By the early 1950's, a scientist argued that the atmosphere of early Earth would have consisted of water vapor, ammonia and methane, and lacking in any oxygen. Still a doctorate candidate at the University of Chicago, **Stanley Miller** set up a flask of water to represent the oceans, connected it to a flask of gases through which he passed electrical charges to mimic lightning. Within a week, several of life's building blocks had turned up in the laboratory and within a month there were spontaneous reactions that produced 13 of the 21 amino acids required for life. Stanley's experiments were described as "the single most significant step in convincing many scientists that life is likely to be abundant" in the universe.

Child Psychology

In the landmark 1954 US Supreme Court decision, Brown v. Board of Education, **Marian Radke-Yarrow**'s well-regarded book "They Learn What They Live" was included as evidence to demonstrate the roots of racial prejudice. Through her career she conducted many influential studies on a range of sensitive issues such as prejudice among elementary school pupils, depression in very young children and evidence of altruism in one-year-olds. Marian spent twenty years observing the interaction between chronically depressed parents and their children and documented the assumption that kids were susceptible to serious depression as they matured.

The Hiss of Jupiter

In the mid 1950's, **Kenneth Franklin** was scanning the skies for radio noise when he heard something that sounded like the hiss from the spark plug of a passing car. Further investigation revealed that it was actually a radio emission from the plant Jupiter, the first sound ever identified as coming from a specific planet. As a result of his work, Kenneth moved on to the Hayden Planetarium in New York City where he spent decades writing and presenting the shows that became an institution, including an annual look at the sky over Bethlehem when Jesus was born. He was also involved with making astronomical calculations for The Farmers Almanac. Although it did not become a commercial success, Kenneth invented a watch for moon walkers that measures time in what he called "lunations", the period it takes the moon to rotate and revolve around the sun.

Butterflies

When you wanted to know anything about butterflies, you went through **Charles Lee Remington**. As a professor at Yale, he helped to shape the field of butterfly research by recruiting and serving as a mentor to several generations of the insect's leading scientists. As a curator at the Peabody museum, Charles established a significant insect collection that is known for its large numbers of specimens and rare holdings—such as the world's largest collection of insects that are part male and part female. He also established the worlds first, and only known, cicada preserve for an insect that appears by the millions only once every 17 years.

Helped Infants Breath

Harvey Colten and his team found a flaw in the gene that is responsible for the normal function of the lungs, a flaw that can lead to respiratory failure and death in some infants. After publishing their findings, they developed a blood test to detect the deficiency and explored alternatives, including lung transplants, as potential remedies for the afflicted children. Transplants were found to be more effective and have been used quite successfully in the past ten years. In his earlier work, Harvey had studied a group of plasma proteins that are important in preparing the body's immune response to infection and aided in describing the protein's function within the bloodstream.

Polio

The vaccine that used the poliovirus in a deactivated form to stimulate an immune response from the affected person was perfected in 1955. Within a seven-year period, reported cases of the virus in the United States dropped from 45,000 a year down to less than 1,000. **Marguerite Vogt** examined how the virus forms in tissue and found that it produced plaques. In collaboration with a colleague who would win the Nobel Prize, she developed methods to determine the extent of polio-infected cells in a given sample of tissue. Marguerite also experimented with animal viruses grown in culture, including the study of how a virus, when introduced to healthy tissue in mice, can change normal cells into cancerous cells.

Fought Tuberculosis

It took two sets of studies by **George Comstock** to determine what did and did not work in the fight against TB. The second series led the health profession to adopt the use of the drug INH as a mainstay in treating tuberculosis, which mainly affects the lungs and remains a leading killer in the world today. In the 1950's, after INH was developed, George moved his family to Alaska that has one of the world's highest rates of TB. After a year of study, INH showed a seventy percent decline in the disease. A follow-up study five years later showed the drug's benefit had been sustained. George also founded the Johns Hopkins Training Center in Maryland and spent 30 years there supervising community-based research studies on cancer, heart disease and a disease of the eye. The center was renamed for him in 2005.

The Benefits of Exercise

The rule of thumb was that for each hour of physical activity, the exerciser gained an extra two hours of life. **Ralph Paffenbarger** in the 1960's began to look at exercise and its effects on 17,000 Harvard graduates ranging in age from their 30's to 70's. He examined sports, walking and stair climbing and translated these exercises into calories that were used up in the course of a week. The findings suggested that men who burned more than

2,000 calories a week faced a significantly lower risk of death from heart disease. The results became a major impetus for the aerobic exercise movement of the 1980's. Ralph was the first recipient in 1996 of the International Olympic Committee prize for sport science.

The Behavior of Cells

When viewed through a light microscope, it was thought that connective tissue that surrounds a cell was nothing more than a large mass. **Elizabeth Hay** harnessed new technologies, while studying the cornea, to show that the molecules in a matrix helped to decide cell behavior, including cell shape, cell-to-cell signaling and tissue function. Her work also helped to promote a better understanding of what connective tissue cells and protective cells contribute to the matrix. Elizabeth also used genetic labeling and video microscopy to explore how cells move. She researched developing embryos with the idea of being able to repair cells that caused deformities, cancer and abnormal wound healing. She was elected to the National Academy of Sciences in 1984.

Free Will

After conducting research on the brain for nearly 20 years, **Benjamin Libet** performed a series of tests that showed the brain starts to respond to a command before a person makes a conscious decision. It suggested that free will is just a method for the mind to justify its actions. Another discovery was that the brain has a very narrow window of opportunity to block those thoughts. Benjamin's approach yielded the only credible evidence of how conscious awareness is produced by the brain. His studies found that there was a consistent half-second delay between the patients' unconscious reaction and their conscious awareness of being stimulated. He felt that his findings demonstrated that a person's will is able to maintain complete control and veto any act it wishes.

The Biochemical Process

As a postgraduate student in the 1960's, **Colin Greenwood** was studying the way carbon monoxide blocked the reaction of oxygen with a complex protein that contains both copper and iron. He knew he could reverse the blockage by flashing bright pulses of light at the protein. Colin realized this technique made it possible to observe the extremely quick reaction of oxygen converting into water. The experiment was recognized as one of the classic pieces of mid-20th century biochemistry and the process became one of the standard methods of measuring ultra-fast biochemical reactions.

Figuring Out the Stars

His groundbreaking work in the quantum mechanics of atoms made decisive contributions to the observation of stars and galaxies. Publishing nearly 300 academic papers, **Michael Seaton** also produced one-of-a-kind observations on collisions between electrons and atoms. He became an expert in programming computers in the mid-1960's during their period of infancy. Remarkably, many programs that were written by his group continue to be developed and remain in use today. While working on problems related to the physics of complex atoms and writing computer code, Michael explored methods to interpret objects in the sky with the help of the newly generated data. The techniques he devised have been used in a multitude of studies, including quasars and the center of the sun. He was considered as one of the greatest specialists in the field of atoms in astrophysics of the last century.

Tissue Engineering

Already in his late 50's, **Eugene Bell**'s years of meticulous research came to the forefront when he mixed human cells, collagen and other ingredients to create a skin-like tissue that could be grafted onto severely injured patients. His work became the basis of an entire generation of studies aimed at regenerating every kind of tissue, from cartilage and bone to nerve and liver. Eugene established two biotechnology companies to make his inventions commercially available. He held over 40 patents on his inventions and authored over 200 papers. In 2003, he received the Biotechnology Achievement of the Year Award from the New York University School of Medicine.

Forgotten Father of the Big Bang

When **Ralph Alpher** was in graduate school in the 1940's, most astrophysicists favored the steady-state theory that promoted the idea that the universe had always existed in its current form and would continue to do so forever. A minority of scientists, at the time, believed that the universe had been created in a massive explosion nearly 14 billion years ago. While still earning his academic credentials, Ralph published papers, based on his calculations, that showed the early universe had undergone an initial cooling phase and the remaining particles had combined to form all of the chemical elements found on earth. He also predicted in his doctoral work that the explosive moment of creation would have released radiation that should still be echoing through space as radio waves. Ralph never received the credit he had earned for his findings and it took until 2007 for him to be awarded the National Medal of Sciences.

Researched T-cells in the Immune System

Edward Boyse was an immunologist who uncovered some important basics of science by publishing the finding that there are functionally different subclasses of T-cells in the immune system—helper and killer T-cells. By examining 100 samples, he was among the first to suggest that umbilical cord blood was a potential source of blood stem cells that could be used for transplant. With others, Edward conducted the first successful cord blood transplant on a French child with a potentially fatal condition. About 10,000 children have since benefited from this procedure. He also looked into the genetics of body odors and found in experiments that mice can tell the difference between relatives and strangers and prefer to mate with partners that are unrelated by blood and smell. Edwards's findings gave rise to the belief that humans have a similar instinct.

ESCA

It means "Electron Spectroscopy for Chemical Analysis" and is used to test the surface of semiconductors, check air samples for impurities and determine the extent of oxidation in a given material. Early attempts to analyze the energy of electrons were largely unsuccessful until **Kai Siegbahn** devised a mushroom-shaped magnet that was able to focus electrons in two directions. This helped to improve the sensitivity of an instrument named the electron spectrograph that revealed a great deal of information about the nature of the nuclei. His efforts changed the spectroscope from being rarely used into a common industrial technique. The son of a Nobel Prize winner, Kai won his own Nobel in 1981 for his work.

Particle Physicist

While a professor at Stanford University, **Wolfgang Panofsky** conducted basic research using high-energy electrons and photons to study the structure and behavior of protons, the fundamental particles at the heart of all atoms. Within a few years, Wolfgang was to lead the planning and building of what was to become the world's first major atom smasher. He was hailed as being the first builder to complete an American government facility anywhere on time and under budget. He also believed that an inventor had an ethical and social responsibility to ensure that their creations were kept in check. Wolfgang encouraged cooperation between the scientists of nuclear-capable countries to work together to lessen the dangers of a nuclear conflict. He was awarded the National Medal of Sciences in 1969.

Ion Thrusters

Until the development of iron propulsion, satellites and deep-space probes could only be launched using conventional rockets. Although they were simple, they were also inefficient and required large amounts of fuel. **David Fearn** was the driving force behind the creation of the iron thruster which enabled telecommunication satellites to be positioned more accurately and made deep space missions possible that were previously not feasible. Thrusters were used in a spacecraft rescue following the failure of a launch rocket and they are slated to be used on the gravity and ocean explorer satellite which will provide a new level of understanding of the planet's composition, climate change processes that operate below the Earth's crust.

Anemia Drug

Anemia causes a decline in red blood cells and interrupts the delivery of oxygen to the body's tissues. About 90% of patients undergoing dialysis for kidney failure become anemic, a condition that was once treated with blood transfusions that could expose them to hepatitis and other diseases. **Joseph Eschbach** looked at various forms of renal failure and the role of a natural hormone, called EPO, in the formation of red blood cells. Joseph and a colleague helped establish that EPO stimulates the production of red cells in bone marrow and could lead to a treatment for anemia in humans. In the 1980's he led a successful clinical trial that developed a synthetic form of the hormone. When the drug was introduced to the marketplace, it led to a difference in patient's well being that was said to be as strong and dramatic as with the advent of the kidney transplant.

Benadryl

Histamines are chemicals made in some cells that can damage the tiny blood vessels called capillaries and allow blood plasma to leak into body tissue to cause swelling, itching and redness. Antihistamines are manufactured compounds that block receptors in the capillaries and prevent the irritating and sometimes even fatal side effects. **George Rieveschl** was a chemical engineer who synthesized a compound that didn't cause drowsiness and resulted in a drug that most people could tolerate. Millions of sufferers of allergies, colds, rashes, hives and hay fevers now swallow a capsule of Benadryl to relieve their symptoms. First on the market in 1946, the patent expired decades ago in 1964 and it is now sold over the counter.

SOCIAL INFLUENCE

Reunited Survivors

When he was twenty the Germans invaded Poland and occupied his native town of Warsaw where **Benjamin Meed** was confined with the city's Jewish population. He eventually escaped and spent World War II helping to smuggle others out of captivity. For decades after the war ended, many Holocaust survivors were isolated and felt disengaged as a community. In 1981 Benjamin helped to convene the first World Gathering of Jewish Holocaust Survivors. The group in Israel attracted 10,000 people followed by another 20,000 two years later in Washington, DC. He helped to reunite people with friends, neighbors and family members that were presumed to have been lost in the war. Benjamin helped establish the US Holocaust Memorial Museum in Washington in 1993 and the Museum of Jewish Heritage in New York City four years later.

Woman NAACP Leader

Her father was born a slave. **Enolia McMillan** took a job as a teacher in the late 1920's and quickly became an advocate for equal pay for black teachers and better schools for black students. By 1935 she had helped to reactivate the Baltimore chapter of the National Association for the Advancement of Colored People (NAACP) and remained an active force with them for more than fifty years. As the 1960's came to a close Enolia was elected president, at age 65, of the Baltimore chapter. By 1986 she had persuaded the NAACP to move its national headquarters to Baltimore and she served as the first female national president for several years. Within the city's school system, she also lobbied successfully against a law that allowed black teachers to be paid less than white teachers.

Ploughshares

The name "Ploughshares" comes from a passage in the book of Isaiah in the Bible that reads, "they shall beat their swords into ploughshares ... neither shall they learn war anymore." **Sally Lilienthal** founded the Ploughshares Fund in 1981 to help prevent the spread and use of nuclear, biological and chemical weapons of war. Since that time, the fund has awarded more than $40 million to groups and individuals, making it one of the largest grant-making foundations in the United States dedicated exclusively to peace and security funding. An early recipient of a Ploughshares grant was the International Campaign to Ban Landmines which received the Nobel Peace Prize in 1997 and helped to bring about a global treaty to abolish antipersonnel landmines. Sally concentrated on giving money to start-up causes, based on the theory that the first grant is always the hardest to get. The group currently gives away about $4 million a year.

Helping the Mentally Ill

Focusing on rehabilitating the whole person and not just their mental illness was the goal of **Marvin Weinstein**. In 1965 he joined the nonprofit mental health agency Portals and helped to develop an approach that was forward thinking for its time: to provide social services in combination with psychiatric rehabilitation to help the mentally ill become productive members of mainstream society. During his 36 years at Portals, Marvin developed a network of programs in the Los Angeles area to help clients obtain housing and jobs while reintegrating into the community. One of his proudest accomplishments was the 1986 launching of Corporate Cookie, a retail cookie stand that now serves more than 1,200 people a month. He also helped to found A Community of Friends, a nonprofit agency that develops affordable housing for the mentally ill homeless.

Influential Author

Discussing rape publicly was still considered taboo in the early 1970's. Back then few women even reported the crime with only an estimated 10% of victims coming forward. During that time, **June Bundy Csida**, and her husband, penned the groundbreaking book "Rape: How to Avoid It and What to Do If You Can't". The book helped to begin a national discussion on social attitudes about rape. The publication was a significant moment in the history of the feminist movement and a noteworthy shift from the public silence surrounding rape. June had joined the National Organization for Women (NOW) in 1970 and used her many contacts to further the goals of the organization and served on its national board of directors.

Open Adoption

Sixty percent of women with unplanned pregnancies gave their children up for adoption in the 1960's. Twenty years later that number was down to three percent due to the legalization of abortion and the increased social acceptance of unwed mothers. Back in the 1940's this type of child was the product of a closed adoption that prevented ties between the birth and adopting parents. The trend toward openness began in the late 1960's when adults who had been adopted demanded to know about their heritage. **Bruce Rappaport** pushed for the right of these parents to choose and know each other decades before it became the norm. His activism began when he was the director of an infertility clinic in the San Francisco area. Bruce and a group of colleagues established a nonprofit adoption center to challenge the thinking of the time. For years his approach was considered cutting edge by combining the speed of independent adoption with counseling for the birth mother and the adopting parents.

Exposed Crime and Corruption

Living the life of a journalist normally does not involve being the focus of assassination attempts. **Jesus Blancornelas** was a pioneering border journalist in Mexico who brought to print the inner workings of Tijuana's murderous drug cartels. As the author of six books, he was considered the leading expert on organized crime and the corruption it brings. He was the first to publish the photo of one of Tijuana's drug lords and he was shot four times by cartel gunmen in an attempt to kill him. Jesus' stories on the corruption of border officials forced him out of three newspapers before he co-founded a weekly newspaper in 1977. In recent years, he was recognized by the United Nations, Reporters Without Borders, the Inter-American Press Society and other groups for his contributions to freedom of expression in a country where reporters are regularly killed for crossing politicians and drug families.

Critic of American Culture

When you turn on a television today it only takes a minute or so to find some channel that is offering news about the world of celebrities. In an image obsessed country, it's difficult to imagine that it was nearly thirty years ago that **George Trow** wrote of the twilight of sophisticated culture that was already taking place in 1980. "Within the Context of No Context" was published in The New Yorker magazine, indicting the emptiness of modern culture that could be traced back to the dumbing down of society from watching television. George believed that meaningful conversation had been devoured by a culture of celebrity driven nonsense. He was a founder of the celebrated National Lampoon magazine and wrote for The New Yorker for 28 years.

An Orphanage in Kenya

The AIDS epidemic in Africa has all but wiped out the middle generation of adults who traditionally would take care of both their older parents and their children. It is estimated that there are more than one million children in Kenya who have been orphaned from both parents dying of AIDS. **Angelo D'Agostino** was a Jesuit priest, as well as a physician, and established "Nyumbani" (home), an orphanage in 1992 that started out with three children. Today, it shelters about 100 children, in age from newborns to a 23 year-old, and has a staff of 76 that includes nurses, teachers, cooks and gardeners. A larger non-profit organization was also formed to provide outreach services to HIV-positive children and their families in the Nairobi area and has the most advanced blood diagnostic laboratory in the country.

A Plaza Mother

During the eight year Argentinean military dictatorship that began in 1976, it was estimated that 13,000 people disappeared during the "Dirty War" against dissidents. Human rights groups put the total closer to 30,000. **Nelva Mendez de Falcone** lost her 16-year-old daughter during this reign of terror when she participated in organizing demands to reduce public transit prices. In 1977, Nelva became one of the first members of the Mothers of Plaza de Mayo who began weekly silent marches on the square in front of the presidential palace, demanding information about missing children. To this day, the Mothers continue to press the government to learn of their fate.

Fought Animal Cruelty

Taking up dairy farming in 1950's England, **Peter Roberts** was so appalled by the treatment of animals in intensive farming systems that he began to write letters to newspapers in protest against the confinement of farm animals in stalls and cages that were too small to permit them to move around. He and his wife set up a trust that became "Compassion in World Farming". When he started out, his vision of an environment in which farm animals were treated with respect and compassion appeared to be hopeless. They were considered agricultural products without any legal protection and his trust was viewed as just another animal welfare campaign being run on emotion. Eventually, his efforts led to a change in the classification of animals under European law from agricultural goods to beings that required humane treatment.

Minority Trailblazer

Judge **Jane Bolin** was the first black woman to graduate from Yale Law School, the first to join the New York City Bar Association, the first to work in the city's legal department and the first black woman in the United States to become a judge when Mayor Fiorello La Guardia appointed her as a family court judge in 1939. When she graduated from Wellesley College in 1928, a guidance counselor told Jane that a career in law for a black woman was virtually nonexistent. At Yale, she was one of only three women and the only black person. While on the bench, she ended the assignment of probation officers on the basis of race and the placement of children in child-care agencies on the basis of ethnic background.

Secret Santa

In the winter of 1971, **Larry Stewart** had just lost his job and was sleeping in his car at night. After two days without food, he ordered a meal at a diner and pretended he had lost his wallet when it was time to pay. The owner dropped a $20 bill on the floor, picked it up, and gave it to Larry as if it were Larry's money. He never forgot that act of generosity. Nearly ten years later, he was laid off yet again and saw a carhop working outside in the cold wearing a jacket that didn't protect her from the chill. Although he was short of money, Larry handed her a $20 and told her to keep the change. For the next 26 years he would take to the streets each Christmas in Kansas City, Missouri and hand out $100 bills. In time, he would become quite wealthy from his ownership of a cable television station and long distance phone service company. In all, it was estimated that he donated more than $1 million anonymously. Larry revealed his identity only a few months before his death in the hope that the publicity would inspire other people toward charitable giving.

Energized France to Help the Homeless

Virtually unknown in the United States, **Abbe Pierre** was voted the third greatest French person of all time by French television viewers in 2005. Although born to wealth, he gave away everything he had and became a monk. The winter of 1954 was a brutally cold time and it had struck the country with terrible consequences. Pierre took to the radio and told stories of a woman being found frozen to death holding an eviction notice in her hands. At that time, twenty percent of the population lived in unacceptable housing. He implored his listeners to do something. Within minutes, volunteers arrived at a relief center and hundreds took to the streets in their cars to find the homeless. Thousands of blankets, tons of clothes and millions of francs were donated. The government, which had earlier turned down his requests, promised 12,000 dwellings. His efforts were later expanded to more than 50 countries on four continents.

A Union's 'Girl Friday"

That's what **Evelyn Munro** called herself while working as a long time activist who fought for sharecroppers' rights in one the United States' first racially integrated labor unions. The Southern Tenant Farmers Union was formed in 1934 to improve working conditions for sharecroppers and tenant farmers in the South. The Union helped set the stage for the civil rights movement thirty years later as a model for social action that united blacks and whites behind a common cause of economic justice. Evelyn supervised the union's headquarters in Memphis, Tennessee and was a trusted associate of the union activist who had co-founded the organization and was its driving force for 20 years. She would often journey on dangerous missions that brought her face to face with lynch mobs and vigilante patrols.

Helped Torture Victims

For eight years **Petra Clark** worked as a volunteer examining doctor at the Medical Foundation for the Care of Victims and Torture. While there, she treated survivors of torture and atrocity and documented their injuries that were used to support asylum claims. Petra sought to change British medical and legal opinion by arguing that politically motivated rape was both torture and a crime. Her lectures and discussions of female anatomy and the after effects of torture moved even the most hardened judges. During her twenty-year tenure at the Department of Health, she pioneered the use of folic acid for pregnant mothers to reduce the risk of spina bifida and its use in general nutrition. She also promoted the Breast is Best campaign and provided new guidelines on feeding the elderly.

Civil Rights Champion

The pursuit of a doctorate in history was abandoned by **Mendy Samstein** in 1964 when he headed to the South to join the historic turmoil of the civil rights movement and gained a reputation as a strong organizer and effective speaker. He helped to recruit and deploy more than 800 mainly white college students who traveled to rural black Mississippi towns as part of the Mississippi Summer Project in '64. Mendy was one of nine committee workers in a house in McComb, Miss. on July 8, 1964 when three blasts ripped the house apart. He became a full-time organizer for the Student Nonviolent Coordinating Committee and black rights leader Stokely Carmichael called him "one in a million".

Father of the Trails System

Outfitted as a Spanish explorer, **George Cardinet, Jr.** led a team of re-enactors on a 900-mile horseback ride in 1976 that snaked north from Mexico through California and closely followed the same trail taken 200 years earlier. George was considered by many to be the father of the California trails system. In the 1940's he had first become interested in trail building when horses began falling out of fashion. He was instrumental in developing the state's first long-distance hiking and equestrian trails and in getting the law passed that established a federal trails system in 1968 which recognized an extensive system of scenic and historic trails across America.

Fought Legal Discrimination

For 27 years **Will Maslow** led the American Jewish Congress in its fight against African-American and Jewish discrimination in employment and housing. His strategy departed from the Jewish community's more conciliatory approach that tried to make changes at the local level through grass roots meetings. Will went to the courts to fight housing restrictions that had made it impossible for Jews to buy property in many American communities and took on colleges and companies that had limits on how many Jews they would admit or hire. In the late 1940's he led a successful lobbying effort to pass a law in New York State that barred discrimination in higher education based on race as well as beliefs or origin. He negotiated with Gertz, the largest department store in Jamaica, Queens, to hire blacks for the first time. Will helped to draft a friend of the court brief in support of the plaintiffs in the landmark 1954 Brown v. Board of Education school desegregation decision.

Saved British Historic Buildings

During a stint on the executive committee of the National Trust in the 1960's, **John Smith** saw the decay and vandalism that had affected many buildings in Britain that had meaning to the history and development of the country. On his own initiative, he founded the Landmark Trust in 1965 based on the idea that people would pay for the privilege of becoming temporary owners of an interesting older building. The income that would be generated would pay for the maintenance. The idea caught on and the trust now owns 184 buildings in Britain as well as a handful in Italy and New England. Among them are forts, mills, towers, gatehouses, railway stations not in use and medieval farmhouses. As part of its mission, Jack promoted a campaign to protect the British coastline.

Gay Activist Since the 50's

It still takes a great amount of courage to come out in public as a gay person. Imagine the stigma when **Barbara Gittings** first announced in the 1950's that she was a lesbian. Over a decade before the Stonewall rebellion of 1969 that started the gay rights movement, she founded the initial East Coast chapter of Bilitis, the first national organization for lesbians. By the 60's she was taking part in early gay rights demonstrations at the White House and other sites. In her most important role, she helped to lobby the American Psychiatric Association to change its stance on homosexuality and they eventually rescinded their definition of being gay as a mental disorder.

Wanted a Better Quality Life for Seniors

When **Clarice Hayman** retired in the 1970's, she not only began preparing for her old age, but for that of aging residents throughout California. She took night courses in gerontology and psychology and transformed herself into an advocate for older people. As a volunteer in the offices of elected officials, she pushed for better nutrition, transportation and recreational services for seniors. Eventually, Clarice won a seat in the California Senior Legislature, which advises the state Legislature and promotes measures to improve the quality of life for older Californians. Her interest was not only in seeing that seniors had services, but also in changing society's perception of old age.

Home for the Poor of India

A meeting with Mahatma Gandhi in the 1940's led British architect **Laurie Baker** to devote his career to building low cost and environmentally sound houses in India. Laurie had sewn together a pair of shoes from discarded scraps and an amused Ghandi challenged him to use the same ingenuity to provide the poor with shelter. He used a technique that utilized perforated screens made with locally manufactured bricks to allow the natural movement of air to cool the interiors of sweltering buildings. His masterpiece was a 10-acre campus built on a hill that combined brick walls wrapped around trees and shade filled courtyards. He was the recipient of the United Nations Habitat Award and the International Union of Architects award.

Breaking the Color Barrier with Pepsi

In the late 1940's, the black consumer was still widely ignored by business in the United States. **Edward Boyd** and a team of well-educated African Americans were hired by Pepsi-Cola to help the company capture the black dollar in its war with Coca-Cola. Edward and his group came up with a groundbreaking ad campaign that featured a black child reaching up to take a bottle of Pepsi from his mother. The ad was one of the first to represent African-Americans as typical Americans. The campaign also included features of stylishly dressed, well-to-do families and black university students. The former chairman and CEO of PepsiCo said that Jackie Robinson may have gotten all of the headlines, but what Ed did was equally groundbreaking.

Examined Race Relations in America

He covered the civil rights movement in the role of a translator. As both a journalist and documentarian, **William Peters** helped the United States learn about itself and its problems. In the 1950's he wrote an article for Redbook magazine and introduced a 27-year-old minister from Atlanta named Martin Luther King, Jr. who was preaching nonviolent resistance. Thirty years later he created the documentary "A Class Divided", for public television, which told the story of a small-town Iowa schoolteacher who had taught her all white class a striking lesson about divisiveness by treating the students differently based on their eye color. This work won William an Emmy in addition to winning four George Foster Peabody awards for other films he made.

The Lenny Bruce of Psychotherapy

His basic message was that all people are born with a talent for "crooked thinking"—distortions of perception that sabotage a basic desire for happiness. **Albert Ellis** also recognized that people had the capacity to change themselves. He felt that the role of a therapist is to intervene directly and help the patient to learn to accept themselves as they are and retrain their behavior to avoid destructive emotions. In popular Friday evening seminars that ran for decades, Albert counseled, prodded, provoked and entertained groups of more than 100 students and psychologists who were looking for answers. He often laced his comments with obscenities for effect. In a 1982 poll of 800 clinical psychologists, Albert was voted the second most influential psychotherapist in history, one notch ahead of Sigmund Freud.

Published the Truth

By 1978 it appeared that the civil rights movement was at an end and a new South had been born. But when **Charles Tisdale** purchased a seemingly innocuous, nearly defunct newspaper that year, the office of the Jackson, Mississippi Advocate was attacked at least 20 times in the years ahead including death threats against Charles, but the paper never missed publishing an issue. The Advocate exposed bribery and corruption among law enforcement officials in the state and brought national attention to a small town that was so poor they lacked indoor plumbing. His muckraking crossed racial lines, skin color did not make a difference while Charles was a strident voice for anyone being treated unfairly.

Foreign Cultures

The Tiv culture was a group of people that lived in Nigeria and were a rarely documented tribe of slash-and-burn farmers under the last days of British rule in the 1950's. Anthropologist **Paul Bohannon** spent four years with the Tiv, living in a mud hut without plumbing and learning their language while documenting their customs and culture. The tribe at the time numbered about 800,000. As the world's leading expert on the Tiv, Paul wrote two books about his experience, one of which included some of the more than 1,200 black and white photos he took during his stay. Separately, he was also known for coining the phrase "the divorce industry". In his book, "All the Happy Families", Paul estimated that the size of the divorce industry rivaled that of the automobile industry and questioned why there weren't similar industries to help families and single parents.

The Rights of Women

It was a law book that brought out the social injustices that women were suffering. **Leo Kanowitz** authored "Women and the Law" in 1969, the first extensive study of women's legal status in the civil rights era. It became a reference work for feminist scholars and activists. He called attention to the fact that the way the law was treating women it could be viewed as a civil right and a human right. The book showed massive evidence of sex-based legal inequality and outlined the differences between men and women in marriage age, minimum wage laws, married names, alimony support and property rights. Leo's work helped proponents of the Equal Rights Amendment bolster their arguments at Congressional hearings although the ERA law was never passed. In 1970, the Los Angeles

Times referred to "Women and the Law" as the most important work in its field.

Fought Bus Segregation Before Rosa Parks

Irene Morgan Kirkaldy's fight against bus discrimination took place a decade before the modern civil rights movement began. In 1944 she was on a Greyhound bus headed to Baltimore from Gloucester County, Virginia when she refused the bus driver's instructions to give up her seat to a white person. Her case was taken up by the NAACP and made its way to the Supreme Court where they ruled in Irene's favor. Her defiance inspired the first freedom ride in 1947 when a group traveled by bus and train to Louisville, Kentucky where they challenged the Southern states to implement the decision in Irene's case. She was honored by Gloucester County, where she had gotten on the bus, on its 350th anniversary. The following year, President Bill Clinton awarded her the Presidential Citizens Medal.

Fought Nuclear Radiation

His groundbreaking work in the 1960's demonstrated that public safety standards for radiation exposure were woefully inadequate. **John Gofman** found that medical x-ray machines and fallout from atomic weapons tests and nuclear power plants posed a far greater cancer risk than was widely believed. In the 1970's he helped found an advocacy group that studied the health effects of ionizing radiation and more recently argued that radiation is overused in medicine for both diagnosis and treatment and doesn't take into account a full consideration of the risks. John also did pioneering work on coronary heart disease where he uncovered and characterized the diversity of proteins in the bloodstream and laid the foundations for continuing studies into what is now known as good cholesterol and bad cholesterol.

Soviet Pollster

In a Communist society where directives came from the top, **Boris Grushin** set out to find what the average person thought. During the

Khrushchev era, Boris founded and edited a paper that conducted the Soviet Union's first public opinion surveys, asking people to identify the major problems in society and getting them to talk about personal matters, including the quality of their marriage and satisfaction with leisure time. The fact that people were asked what they thought was revolutionary in a totalitarian society. Boris oversaw the first large study of public attitudes in a single Soviet city and during the Gorbachev years he established a center for public opinion studies that was free to raise politically charged questions. By 1993 he had become an adviser to President Boris Yeltsin of Russia.

SPORTS

Free Climber

His rock climbing methods promoted the use of no artificial instruments to advance on a climb and called for the aid of ropes and other equipment as safety devices only when a fall takes place. **Todd Skinner** set a new course for climbing when he rejected the traditional approach of returning to the bottom to start over after a fall. He practiced the tactic of "hangdogging" in which he hung from his rope and repeated a move several times before moving forward with the climb. Todd made ascents on dozens of the world's most treacherous climbs. His most renowned feat was scaling the "Nameless Tower" in the Himalayan range in Pakistan, a 4,700-foot rock face that no one had ever tried to free climb. In all, Todd claimed to have made 300 first ascents in 30 countries that helped to establish his reputation as one of the most well-rounded climbers in the world.

The Kentucky Derby

"And they're off" is the familiar refrain for horse racing announcers everywhere. In order for the horses to be off and running someone has to let them out of the gate. **Tom Wagoner** had the honor of releasing the horses for the running of the Kentucky Derby for 24 years. Beginning with the 100th running in 1974, it was Tom's duty to hit the button to open the gate doors. He was known as "Quick Draw" to many jockeys for scanning the field as the last horse entered the gate to make sure all the horses were looking down the track. Tom would say "if the heads are straight, usually the butts will follow". Among the races he started were the beginning of the Triple Crown runs for Seattle Slew in 1977 and Affirmed the following year, the only back-to-back Triple Crown winners in history.

Hungarian Soccer Great

Known as the "Galloping Major" during his heyday in the 50's and 60's, **Ferenc Puskas** was one of the most charismatic and finest players in international soccer history. A gold medal winner at the Helsinki Olympics in 1952, Ferenc was the outstanding star on the legendary Hungarian national team whose only loss during one six year period was to West Germany in the final of the 1954 World Cup. The team was called the "Magical Magyars" and Ferenc was considered to be their most gifted magician. It was said that he had a seventh sense for soccer and in 1999 he was voted the sixth best soccer player of the 20th century.

Overcame Disease to Excel in Tennis

Juvenile Type I diabetes can be life threatening if not handled properly. At the age of 15, **Ham Richardson** was diagnosed with the disease when he was one of the best junior tennis players in the United States. He went to several doctors who told him he would never play again until he found one that said it was okay to continue. He went on to become the number one ranked player in the US in 1956 and '58, winning 17 national titles and playing on seven Davis Cup teams. When he won the French junior championship, he had to spend every night at a Paris hospital while doctors tried to stabilize his fluctuating blood sugar levels. He passed out as a result of low blood sugar on the way to a party the evening before he was to play in the finals of a different tournament, then won the championship the next day.

Dog Show Judge

At 6 feet 2 inches, **Anne Rogers Clark** was an imposing and instantly recognizable presence in the dog show ring. For six decades, she was a fixture at Westminster and holds many records. Among them, she was the first woman to win best in show as a professional handler and she ranked second among all handlers with three best in shows. She also shared the record for most judging appearances at Westminster with 22. A handler, a judge and a breeder, Anne was a walking encyclopedia on the standards of more than 400 breeds worldwide and was one of only two dozen people licensed to judge all 165 breeds and varieties recognized by the American Kennel Club. She attended every Westminster Kennel club show since 1941.

Pitchin Paul

Although he wasn't good enough to make his high school basketball team, **Paul Arizin** would later be named the college player of the year by The Sporting News, be elected to the Basketball Hall of Fame and earn the distinction of being named one of the 50 best players in the history of the NBA. When he joined the Philadelphia Warriors in 1950, the game was slow moving and primarily featured set shots. The 24-second clock was still several years away. He didn't invent the jump shot, but Paul refined it and became one of the league's first jump shot specialists. He admitted it came about by accident. Some of the games were played on dance floors that became slippery. When he tried to hook, his foot would go out from under him so he began to jump. Since his feet weren't on the floor he no longer had to be concerned with slipping. Practice made perfect and not too long afterward he found that nearly all of his shots had become jump shots.

AFL Founding Father

In 1959, **Lamar Hunt** had been unsuccessful in acquiring an NFL franchise for Dallas, where he lived. Not content with their decision, he decided to form a rival league that would begin play the following year and worked out the basics of the plan on an airplane letterhead during a flight. His new team, the Dallas Texans, would relocate to Kansas City a few years later, and become the Chiefs, after the NFL decided to put a new team there (the Cowboys) after all. He would continue to own the team for 47 years. When the two leagues decided to merge in 1966, Lamar had a lead role in representing the NFL. When it came time to decide on a name for the championship game between the two leagues he came up with the Super Bowl. He said it was in his head that his son had been playing with a then quite popular toy called a super ball and he changed the name slightly to describe the title game. Today, the American Football Conference championship trophy is named after Lamar.

One of the First and Best Female Golfers

The numbers all add up: starting in 1922, **Maureen Orcutt** won more than 65 major ladies golf tournaments with the first coming at the age of 19 and the last at the age of 61. She not only played against the best women golfers, but also played in exhibitions against the best male professionals too. Twice she was runner up for the U.S. amateur title. In 1969 she received the first Tanqueray Award for contributions to amateur sports and was elected to the World Golf Hall of Fame and the New York Sports Hall of Fame. Her trendsetting went beyond the field of sports competition. In 1937 she began to cover women's golf and write a column called "Women in Sports" for The New York Times while becoming one of the first female sportswriters for a major newspaper. For years, she was the only woman among fifty men in the sports department.

The King and His Court

It's hard to imagine one pitcher striking out 141,516 batters in a career, but that's what **Eddie Feigner** did over a 60-year period. Eddie and his four man softball team traveled around the world on barnstorming tours while logging over 4 million miles, 100 countries and playing before 200 million people. They would play at racetracks, rodeos, pastures, cemeteries and oilrigs. With his 100-mile-an-hour pitches, Eddie could pitch behind his back, from second base, between his legs, kneeling and blindfolded. He threw 930 no-hitters and 238 perfect games. In a nationally televised exhibition in 1964 at Dodger Stadium, Eddie struck out Willie Mays, Willie McCovey, Maury Wills, Harmon Killebrew, Roberto Clemente and Brooks Robinson in order. Sports Illustrated called him the most underrated athlete of his time. In 2002, ESPN.com listed Eddie as one of the ten greatest pitchers in a list that also included Walter Johnson and Sandy Koufax.

Track and Field Olympian

She started out in the Mississippi Delta cotton fields and competed in every Olympics from 1956 through 1972, becoming the first and only American track and field athlete to compete in five Olympics. Only an injury kept **Willye White** off the 1976 team. She won a silver medal in the long jump in 1956 when she was a 16-year-old high school sophomore and took a second silver in a meter relay eight years later. She was America's best female long jumper for almost twenty years and won nine consecutive US outdoor championships and competed in 150 countries. Sports Illustrated for Women named Willye one of the 100 greatest women athletes of the 20th century.

Fought the Reserve Clause

He was way before his time. While pitching for the St. Louis Cardinals in the 1940's, **Max Lanier** jumped to the newly established Mexican Baseball League that had no affiliation with Major League Baseball in the US. The incentive for Max was an offer to double his salary plus a bonus for a five-year period. He joined a dozen other major leaguers who made the move south of the border. Broken contract promises, poor playing conditions and an unfamiliar culture led to a change of mind. Max tried to return to the Cardinals 18 months later, but was barred by the commissioner of baseball, Happy Chandler, who had dished out five-year suspensions against every player that had jumped leagues. Max filed a suit in federal court maintaining that baseball had violated antitrust laws by depriving them of their livelihood and challenged the longstanding reserve clause that tied players to their teams for as long as owners wanted them. Faced with a challenge to baseball's long held contract structure, Chandler lifted the suspensions and the lawsuit was dropped. It would take nearly 25 years for the reserve clause to be eliminated and free agency to be introduced. The result was a salary windfall for future players that Max, and players of earlier generations, was never able to enjoy.

Ski Jumping

An adjustment to an injured shoulder changed the course of the sport of ski jumping. **Eric Windisch** tried to protect himself from that injury during a tournament in Germany in 1949 by leaving his slightly arched arms pointing downward. To his surprise, and to the on looking competitors and spectators, he soared farther than anyone else. The traditional position was to have your arms forward, in a Superman type pose. There had been variations in style since ski jumping had started in Norway in the late 1800's, but this was considered as the benchmark event. Eric's newly created position had an aerodynamic advantage that was demonstrated in wind tunnel tests. The other practical reason for its popularity was that it happened at a large European meet that was well attended by the sport's movers and shakers.

Shot-Putter

When **Parry O'Brien** first began his shot-put career at the University of Southern California in the early 1950's, it was typical to stand at the rear of the seven-foot-ring, hop, turn 90 degrees and push out the 16-pound iron ball. After a tough loss, Parry went home and experimented with a 180-degree turn. The move became known as the "O'Brien Glide". Before the change he couldn't put the shot more than 55 feet. After that, he would go on to break the world record 17 times in a 13-year period with a best of 63 feet, 3 inches. He won two gold medals and one silver at three Olympic games and was so well respected he carried the American flag in the opening ceremonies of the 1964 Tokyo Games. Parry was a member of the US Track and Field Hall of Fame as well as the US Olympic Hall of Fame.

College Football Coaching Legend

During a phenomenal 55 years as the head coach at Grambling State University, **Eddie Robinson** was the first to reach the 400 win plateau and sent scores of players to the NFL. Most importantly, he helped bring racial awareness to a segregated Southern society by barnstorming throughout the South, and the country, to promote his football program and college of 5,000 students in Louisiana. At one point in the early 1970's, there were 43 former Grambling players in NFL training camps. In all, more than 200 players went into the professional ranks. His total of 408 wins ranks second all-time for a college football coach at any level of play.

Hiking Icon

It was said he was to backpacking what Jack Kerouac had been to road trips. Well respected for his lyrical and practical writings on hiking, **Colin Fletcher** became one of the first to walk the length of the Grand Canyon. His book, "The Complete Walker", is an exhaustive guide to outdoors travel that is generally regarded as the backpacker's bible. He offered practical advice on how to arrange campsites, cook meals and pack a knapsack in order to reduce the weight of every item that required carrying. Published forty years ago, it remains in print and has sold more than 500,000 copies.

Hot Air Ballooner

In the autumn of 1960, **Ed Yost** strapped himself into what resembled a lawn chair that was attached to an orange nylon balloon. Igniting the propane tanks to heat air that had been pumped by a fan into the balloon, he lifted off. With that ascent, Ed became known as the father of modern hot air ballooning. The sport now has thousands of followers around the world. Among his feats were measuring cosmic rays in the stratosphere, crossing the English Channel and barely missing becoming the first balloonist to cross the Atlantic by coming within 700 miles of Portugal. Ed held 26 patents dealing with hot air ballooning, including inflation mechanisms, balloon body structures and gondola designs. He was the first inductee into the National Ballooning Hall of Fame.

Developed NASCAR

When he took over the helm from his father in the early 1970's, **Bill France, Jr.** faced a NASCAR operation that had a regional appeal with events only appearing on television as excerpts, primarily on Wide World of Sports. In time, it would become a stunning marketing success, drawing national audiences second only to the NFL. With cars bunched tightly together and exceeding speeds of 200 miles an hour, most cars could generate 750 horsepower, cost $75,000 and last only one race. When Bill expanded the reach of the sport, he decided to take NASCAR nationwide and developed the Winston Cup season championship with a points system that required star drivers to compete in every race to win the title. By 2003, merchandise sales for the sport had reached $2 billion a year.

Babe Ruth of Rodeo

He said they hadn't even invented concussions when he was riding bucking broncos and snorting bulls. **Jim Shoulder**'s was a 16-time world champion rodeo cowboy and a leading figure in the Calgary Stampede and Cheyenne Frontier Days Rodeo as well as being a central attraction at the rodeo's annual appearance at Madison Square Garden in New York. He represented the sport at all rungs, including winning championships as a bull rider and bareback rider. Once, a bull hit him in the face and broke 27 bones. Featured in a Life Magazine photo shoot in 1961, Jim was referred to as "Mister Broken Bones". It was well recognized that he helped to set the stage for taking rodeo to the next level where more people accepted it as a sport.

Indoor Tennis

The cold harsh winters of the Midwest are not agreeable to the refined outdoor game of tennis. Armories and gymnasiums would serve as host courts, but the atmosphere just wasn't what it needed to be. **Jerry Schneider** wanted to build an indoor tennis facility with a pro shop, locker room and other amenities for dues paying members and operate it like a health club. Once he got financial backing, he put up the country's first indoor tennis facility in 1961 in a Chicago suburb that featured asphalt floors, indoor lighting and four courts. Before long, the number of courts doubled and a sauna and exercise room was added. Jerry's concept preceded the sport's boom in the 1960's and '70's and once prompted Tennis magazine to dub him "the father of modern indoor tennis".

Discus Champion

When he was in high school, **Al Oerter** was a sprinter and then a miler on the track team. One day a discus landed near his feet and he casually threw it back so far that the coach immediately made him a discuss thrower. He became a national schoolboy record holder and set in motion a career that saw him win four consecutive Olympic titles, the first modern track and field athlete to do so in one event. Each time he was not the favorite, but still wound up setting an Olympic and world record. In an era before elite track athletes trained year round and some received lucrative endorsement contracts, Al worked full time as a computer executive while competing during his free time.

Hot Rods

What began as a dead-of-night outlaw adventure has turned into a nationally televised sport with millions in annual prize money. **Wally Parks** began racing a modified 1924 Chevrolet in a dry lakebed in California in the 1930's. From there he joined one of the country's first hot-rod car clubs, but they began to take heat from racing incidents on city streets. Using a strip of land on what is now John Wayne Airport in Southern California, it became the first to charge admission for races in that area. With no set rules, Wally determined that a quarter-mile was enough room to run a full race. As editor of Hot Rod magazine, he was instrumental in holding the first sanctioned races for the sport. The National Hot Rod Association is now the world's largest promoter of professional drag racing with 80,000 members and 35,000 licensed competitors sponsoring competitions at 140 tracks in North America. Wally was a member of the International Motorsports Hall of Fame in both Alabama and Michigan.

TECHNOLOGY

Docking System

His first job was working for the designer who sent the world's first artificial satellite into space. When the Russians launched Sputnik in 1957 a seismic shift occurred in making outer space the new destination for technology to prosper. **Vladimir Syromyhatnikov** in the 1970's would create a docking system to link the Soviet Soyuz and US Apollo space capsules, a system that is still in use today. In the 1990's he updated it for the meeting of the Mir space station and the Atlantis shuttle at the International Space Station. Vladimir's docking system and his other designs of onboard manipulators and solar arrays that can be reused are considered to be among the jewels of the Russian space program.

Pioneering Sound Engineer

A passion for the spoken word in radio and television broadcasts encouraged **Desmond Briscoe** to experiment with sound effects in dramatic productions and collaborate with writers and directors to introduce electronic and acoustic sounds into their work. In Samuel Beckett's first radio play in 1957, Desmond created a new "pure radio" by making music from editing and manipulating bits of prerecorded magnetic tape and creating sounds that had never before been heard on British radio. It brought about a breakthrough in bringing to the public's attention the potential for electronic tape effects in drama.

Developed the Disk Drive

It seemed as if **Alan Shugart** was intimately involved at every important juncture of the computer storage industry for more than four decades. During that time storage systems shrank from monsters the size of large washing machines to compact boxes that could fit in your hand while dig-ital storage capacities soared from the equivalent of several books to whole libraries. In the 1950's, Alan helped to develop the first disk drive, named the Ramac (random access method of accounting and control) which could store five million characters of data. During his time at IBM, one of the products he managed in development was a system that became the basis for Sabre, the country's first online reservation system that was cre-ated for American Airlines. By the late 1970's Alan helped to found Seagate Technology that became the first maker of the 5.25 hard disk and swept away business use of floppy disks.

Airplane Safety

A holder of more than 200 patents, **Leonard Greene** founded Safe Flight Instrument in 1946 and developed a device that warns pilots when their plane is about to stall. Over six decades, more than a half million of the instruments have been sold. The device sounds an alert when the plane is in danger of not having the lift it needs to stay aloft and gives the pilot time to take corrective action. It has become standard equipment on planes, both large and small, and has helped to reduce the number of acci-dents that occur as the result of a stalled plane. Leonard was also co-founder of the Corporate Angel Network, an organization that arranges free rides for cancer patients traveling for treatment.

Electron Microscope

The original electron microscope could magnify objects about 1,500 fold, but it had significant problems. **James Hillier**'s first version was capable of 7,000 fold and later improvements by him and others brought it up to a million-fold and made it possible to put blood cells and bacteria under the microscope without burning them up from the power of the electron beam. Also possessing a salesperson's touch, he sold 50 instruments, within two years in the 1940's, at $10,000 apiece and developed 50 pio-neers in 50 different fields. For his work, James was awarded the presti-gious Lasker Award for basic medical research in 1960. Today, the electron microscope is a common tool used in laboratories throughout the world.

The Character of Sound

The roots of his work came from his own life experience. **Daniel Raichel** suffered from severely impaired hearing since childhood and he wore a hearing aid throughout his life. He became a mechanical engineer and an expert on acoustics who studied how sound travels in such varied venues as symphony halls and industrial workplaces. In addition to teaching acoustical theory and noise control at Cooper Union and the Pratt Institute in New York City, he worked as a consultant on sound in the aerospace and electronics industries. Earlier in his career, Daniel conducted noise studies at airports and construction sites, helped design stereo speakers and looked at how equipment sent into space might better withstand vibrations. A book on acoustics that he authored in 2000 is considered to be one of the best surveys on the subject.

Designed Software for Supercomputers

Early computers were based on a single processor that would perform the steps of a software program in sequence. By the 1970's and 80's, researchers began to look for ways to increase computing speed by harnessing up to thousands of processors. The challenge was the need to create a program that would make it easy to use such complex machines. **Ken Kennedy** developed a software technology that served as the foundation for successive generations of scientists and engineers who were able to create advanced simulations that included weather and climate predictions and car collisions. In a 2003 analysis, a programming association identified five of Ken's research papers as among the fifty most influential papers of the past twenty years. No other scientist had more than three.

Lowriders

During World War II there were no cars made in the United States. The automobile factories were used to produce tanks and land vehicles for the war effort. With veterans returning home after the war ended, they came

back with acquired skills and money that led them to experiment and customize used cars. A low-rider car can ride low, they can ride high and they
can hop. **Julio Ochoa Ruelas** was a co-founder and the first president of
Dukes Southern California, the oldest low-rider car club in continuous
existence in the world. He promoted the best of low-rider life by spending
40 years heading a car club that now has 29 chapters. Julio and his brother
were honored by the manufacturer of car care products, Meguiar's, in
2004 as "Treasures of the Hobby" for encouraging low riding as a sport
and establishing family-oriented car clubs around the world.

Created the Couch Potato

It's hard to believe that the television remote control was invented back in
1956. **Robert Adler** was a physicist at Zenith Electronics when he and a
fellow engineer created the Space Command ultrasonic remote control.
Using a high-frequency sound, a sound wave was generated by hitting a
spring-loaded button that produced a clicking sound when it was pushed.
It became the standard of the television industry for 25 years with Zenith
selling 9 million remotes until the current device using infrared signals
began to dominate the market in the early 1980's. Robert's efforts were
not confined to the TV remote, he held nearly 200 US patents and prided
himself most for the work he did on improving television reception by
reducing electromagnetic interference. In 1997, Robert was awarded an
Emmy for his co-invention of the remote.

The M.R.I.

Magnetic resonance has revolutionized medicine by giving it a clear look
inside the vulnerable human body without cutting it open and avoiding
unneeded surgery and the effects of radiation from X-rays. MRI relies on the
magnetic properties of the hydrogen contained in water that makes up two-
thirds of the human body. When the hydrogen atoms are placed in a powerful magnetic field and bombarded with radio waves, they emit radio signals
that provide information about the area around it. Even the brain is now
becoming an open book, as refinements have allowed researchers to identify
which parts are active during different mental tasks. **Paul Lauterbur**'s work

as a physicist played a key role in its development. First available in 1973, its use has exploded to where more than 60 million MRI exams are performed each year. Paul shared the 2003 Nobel Prize in Medicine for his revolutionary efforts.

Fortran

In the 1950's, computers had no software. In order to use it, researchers had to input code instructions by hand. Weary of coding hardware by hand, **John Backus** pitched an idea to his bosses at IBM to create a team to come up with a way to simplify lines of instructions with "loops", or instructions that are automatically created by simple commands. The team worked to find a way to make the machines more useful for scientists and mathematicians. By 1957 they had developed Fortran, which stood for Formula Translation, and became the language for scientific computing and resembled a combination of English shorthand and algebra. What had previously taken 1,000 machines to get the work done now took just 47. John would later earn a National Medal of Science and the top honor from the National Academy of Engineering.

The Laser

Before the advent of the laser came the maser which depended on microwave energy. When it was suggested that a device could use visible light to concentrate and intensify electromagnetic energy, a mad scramble took place among many scientific laboratories to win a $50,000 prize, big money in 1960. **Theodore Maiman** won the race by using rubies to stimulate the energy. The first laser was tiny, compared to later models, but it shone with the brilliance of a million suns. Lasers are machines that amplify light waves of atoms that have been stimulated to radiate, and then shoot them out as narrow, intense beams of light. They are used, among many other purposes, to read CD's and bar codes, guide missiles, remove ulcers, fabricate steel and precisely measure the distance from Earth to the Moon. Theodore was twice nominated for the Nobel Prize and was a member of the National Inventors Hall of Fame.

The Schoolboy Pilot

Fired up by the exploits of Charles Lindbergh, **Robert Buck** built a glider and took to the air at the age of 15. Three years later he had set 14 junior aviation records, including the transcontinental airspeed record. He was recognized as a child prodigy, going aloft in one-seaters, dressed in leather helmet and goggles and flying without the use of a radio. In 1930 he set out to break the junior speed record for a coast-to-coast flight. Armed with six chocolate bars and a canteen of water, he pedaled his bicycle to the airport in Newark because he wasn't old enough to drive a car. By the age of 20 he had flown a light plane higher than anyone had before and photographed the ancient ruins of the Yucatan from the air for the first time. His book, "Weather Flying", which Robert wrote in 1970, is considered required reading for pilots.

Critic of Technology's Basics

Systems analysis uses math models to perform cost-benefit analyses and risk assessments on complex technologies like radar systems and military planes. It came into prominence after World War II and caused **Ida Hoos** to speak up in protest at its inability to see the results it had in social situations. She wanted to see systems analysis balanced with considerations given to the effect it had on the work force. A process that relied solely on numbers when it impacted people was not acceptable without looking beyond dry data on a page. A sociologist, Ida was seen as the intellectual conscience in the field of technology assessment and was known to never accept superficial answers or evasive arguments.

Superconductors

In different forms, they're used in computers, electrical generators, medical equipment and other applications. **Donald Ginsburg** grew crystals in his laboratory and studied their ability to conduct electricity with great efficiency when heated to high temperatures. By doing so, he helped to establish a process that allowed the crystals to grow to a state of exceptional purity. Donald distributed his results to his fellow researchers at the University of Illinois and other institutions around the world and became a leading expert on the production and functioning of supercomputers.

Three Timer

Many astronauts flew during the 'glory years' of NASA in the 1960's, but only one was able to be a member of all three of the premier Mercury, Gemini and Apollo space programs. **Wally Schirra** was one of the original Mercury Seven astronauts, the fifth American in space and the third American to orbit the earth. He participated in the first rendezvous in space with another orbiting spacecraft when its success depended on whether the Apollo program was going to advance and land men on the moon. On his final mission, Wally and his crew orbited the Earth 163 times and provided the first televised pictures from a space capsule. By the end of the decade he had received the Robert Collier Trophy, the highest honor for achievement in aviation.

Designed Deep Sea Vessel

A submersible vehicle used to be limited because of its mechanics. Jacques Cousteau once used one and it could only function in shallow water because deep diving craft had restricted mobility from being so heavy. **Bud Froehlich**'s knowledge of creating small spheres able to endure hostile environments was crucial to his success in building the Alvin, a deep-sea research vessel. Initially, it was able to take two passengers 6,000 feet underwater. In later years, with a stronger titanium shell, it could reach depths of more than 14,000 feet. The Alvin was used to find previously undiscovered aquatic life near intensely hot sea vents 7,000 feet down off of the Galapagos Islands. Its crowning achievement was a trek to the North Atlantic in 1986 to find the Titanic, which rested more than 12,000 feet under water.

Early Satellites

In 1957, the Soviet Union pulled off a public relations coup by being the first nation to send a satellite into space. Caltech engineer **Homer Stewart** took a leave of absence to help the United States prepare for the launch of

Explorer I, the initial rocket that the US successfully launched. He went before the Senate in 1959 to explain how far ahead the Russians had become in their plans for conquering outer space. Homer was named the director of planning at NASA and specialized in determining how to get a rocket into space and enter the correct orbit. It was Homer who recommended Cape Canaveral in Florida as the launching site for space bound craft. His contributions continued with his recommendations for what would become the Apollo missions to the Moon.

Halogen Lamp

Designing, making and importing lamps was **George Kovacs**' career. He introduced popular table lamps, floor lamps, hanging pendants and wall scones. It was in the early 1970's that he brought out the first American-made halogen torchiere—a lamp on a tall pole with a small head holding a slender quartz bulb. The very hot bulb could last an extremely long time and bounce enough light off of the ceiling to light the entire room. Halogens were first rolled out in Europe a decade earlier, but it was only after George began to make them that other manufacturers caught on and began to market their own variation. One of his most popular designs was a creation called the 'Save Your Marriage' lamp that had twin adjustable lights attached to the same plate above the bed.

Old Technology

With technology's ability today to perform, it seems, almost any function, **Ray Erlenborn**'s job is a real throwback. In the earlier days of radio and television, no one pushed a button to make a sound effect, they were all generated by hand. The best sound effects people were artists and performers who had the talent to work together with actors on timing and emphasis. Whether it was a dog barking or a door slamming shut, you had to be on the mark to get the desired, natural sounding result. On radio, Ray could be heard creating effects for such legendary shows as "Amos 'n' Andy", "Burns and Allen" and Edgar Bergen and Charlie McCarthy. On television, he was behind the scenes on "The Jack Benny Show", "The Red

Skeleton Show", "Playhouse 90", "The Sonny and Cher Comedy Hour" and "The Carol Burnett Show".

Artificial Intelligence

It began with Menace, a game-playing machine consisting of 300 matchboxes and a collection of glass beads of different colors that could play tick-tack-toe. It proved that a machine could learn from past games and stored memory. The next step for **Donald Michie** was Freddy, a computer driven robotic arm that could choose and assemble parts. His breakthroughs gained wide recognition after industries in Japan began to use robotic machines in manufacturing in the 1980's. Artificial intelligence and machine learning were popular research topics in the 1960's and '70's with attention focused on computer vision, robotics, machine translation and expert systems that could deal with limited amounts of information. Donald also wrote computer programs that have been used to improve flight simulators for pilot training and increase the efficiency of a uranium refining plant.

Locating People More Easily

The first city directories in the United States were published as far back as the 1780's and were arranged alphabetically by last name with a few organized by street address. For 150 years after that, the publishers would send their researchers from door to door, manually recording the names of residents in every building on every block in the city. **Jack Cole** found a better way by using IBM punch cards in the late 1940's to turn the phone book into a searchable database. Known as crisscross, or reverse, directories, the Cole Directory listed a city's residents by address as well as by phone number. The directory became a staple of public library reference shelves and greatly aided the advertising efforts of business, both large and small.

Radio Telescopes

In 1961, **Ronald Bracewell** built a complex of 32 radio telescope dishes near the Stanford University campus that monitored the surface of the sun for 11 years, producing daily maps of its temperature as well as images of the shape and surface temperatures of stars and other matter in the galaxy. The maps were instrumental in helping to predict the solar storms that disrupt radio communications on Earth. The complex math process that Ronald devised to extract images from radio signals was later on used by other scientists to develop X-ray images of tumors and other forms of medical imaging that scan electromagnetic and radio waves. The images are now widely used in CT and MRI imaging in medicine.

Brought Innovation to Concert Halls

Looking to the past for inspiration, **Russell Johnson** took basic principles from the great 19th-century concert halls of Europe. The ones most cherished by musicians had certain elements in common—they had no more than 2,000 seats and a shoe box shape. To this Russell added such features as sound cushioned canopies above the orchestra, reverberation chambers with doors that open and close and a system of motorized curtains that could be adjusted to customize the sound quality of a room. He strove to achieve four acoustic qualities: loudness, warmth, clarity and echo. Russell completed more than 140 projects over a nearly 40-year period while designing concert halls throughout the world.

The Gossamers

Circling hawks and vultures were the objects of his study. An accomplished meteorologist, a world-class glider pilot and a respected aeronautical engineer, **Paul MacReady** headed the team that built two flimsy, awkward-looking planes powered by a pedaling bike racer. The Gossamer Condor and the Gossamer Albatross, the first successful human-powered planes, along with other imaginative projects, led to more than 30 prestigious awards, including the Collier Trophy for achievement in aeronautics and astronautics, and five honorary degrees. In 1980, Paul was named Engineer of the Century by the American Society of Mechanical Engineers. Today, the Gossamer Condor hangs from a ceiling, next to Charles Lindbergh's Spirit of St. Louis, in the Smithsonian Air and Space Museum in Washington, DC.

Prolific Inventor

Known as one of the grandfather of polymer chemistry, **Norman Gaylord** founded a research institute in 1961 and went on to hold 300 domestic and foreign patents. He was a consultant to over 100 companies and specialized in resins, rubbers, fibers and plastics. Polymer chemistry is the science of stringing molecules together for practical use. He created scratch-resistant material for airplane windshields and was best known for developing a gas permeable hard contact lens that allowed oxygen to reach the eye and prevent swelling and blurred vision, a common problem for hard contact wearers. Norman published more than 250 technical articles and five books.

How Machines Learn

Devising an early computer system that could recognize handwriting, **Ryszard Michalski** expanded the field of machine learning by creating applications in which computers could execute a form of reasoning, drawing conclusions from information supplied to them. His specialty is similar to, but distinct from, artificial intelligence. The underlying purpose of much of Ryszard's work was to use computers to recognize patterns that could ease the decision-making process in seemingly unrelated systems. Among the fields his research has been applied to are agriculture, medicine, the stock market, fraud protection and voice recognition.

Standardized Camera Equipment

It started out as a film-development lab in his parent's bathroom and turned into a multi-million dollar business. Because of his business success and his relentless approach, **Fred Spira** influenced the standardization of photographic accessories and the trend toward making the gadgets more affordable. He was responsible for the fish-eye lens, which can take a wide, hemispheric image and for the increase in lenses that can be switched from one camera to another. His system of interchangeable lens mounts was accepted by manufacturers in the US, Japan and Russia. With his son, Fred wrote "The History of Photography as Seen Through the Spira Collection" in 2001 which traced its technological development. The study was based on his collection of 10,000 books, articles and documents that were written by or about prominent figures in photographic history. The collection also included 20,000 photographic devices including one of the earliest known outdoor photos, a daguerreotype of a country road.

Honor Roll

	Born	Died	Age
Robert Adler	Vienna, Austria	Boise, ID	93
Antonio Aguilar	Zacatecas, Mexico	Mexico City	88
Robert Altman	Kansas City, MO	Los Angeles	81
Ralph Alpher	Washington, DC	Austin, TX	86
Momofuku Ando	Taiwan	Osaka, Japan	96
M. Antonioni	Ferrara, Italy	Rome, Italy	94
Bois Sec Ardoin	Duralde, LA	Eunice, LA	91
Paul Arizin	Philadelphia	Philadelphia	78
Rudolf Arnheim	Berlin, Germany	Ann Arbor, MI	102
Edmund Arnold	Bay City, MI	Salem, VA	93
Robert Austrian	Baltimore, MD	Philadelphia, PA	90
John Backus	Philadelphia, PA	Ashland, OR	82
Roger Bacon	Cleveland, OH	Oberlin, OH	80
Albert Baez	Puebla, Mexico	Redwood City, CA	94
Laurie Baker	Birmingham, England	Kerala, India	90
Joseph Barbera	New York City	Los Angeles	95
Jean Baudrillard	Reims, France	Paris	77
Eugene Bell	New York City	Boston, MA	88
Cuesta Benberry	Cincinnati, OH	St. Louis, MO	83
Ingmar Bergman	Uppsala, Sweden	Faro, Sweden	89
Ruth Bernhard	Berlin, Germany	San Francisco	101
Jesus Blancornelas	San Luis Potosi, Mexico	Tijuana, Mexico	70

	Born	*Died*	*Age*
Henry Beachell	Waverly, NE	Pearland, TX	100
Leonard Berg	St. Louis, MO	St. Louis, MO	79
John Billings	Melbourne, Australia	Melbourne, Australia	89
Braguinha	Rio de Janeiro	Rio de Janeiro	99
Paul Bohannan	Lincoln, NE	Visalia, CA	87
Jane Bolin	Poughkeepsie, NY	New York City	98
Edward Boyd	Riverside, CA	Los Angeles	92
Edward Boyse	Worthing, England	Tucson, AZ	83
Ronald Bracewell	Sydney, Australia	Stanford, CA	86
Edward Brandt	Oklahoma City, OK	Oklahoma City, OK	74
William Bright	Oxnard, CA	Louisville, CO	78
Desmond Briscoe	Birkenhead, England	London	70
Joel Brodsky	New York City	Stamford, CT	67
Ruth Brown	Portsmouth, VA	Henderson, NV	78
Theodore Brunner	Nuremberg, Germany	Laguna Beach, CA	72
Robert Buck	Elizabethport, NJ	Berlin, VT	93
Neville Butler	Harrow, England	London	86
Job Bwayo	Bungomas, Kenya	Nairobi, Kenya	58
Maureen Cannon	New York City	Wyckoff, NJ	84
George Cardinet	San Francisco	Mexico City	97
Bob Carroll, Jr.	McKeesport, PA	Los Angeles	88
Dwight Chamberlain	Rochester, NY	Leota, IN	68
Alfred Chandler	Guyencourt, DE	Cambridge, MA	88
Stella Chess	New York City	New York City	93
Anne Clark	New York City	Greenwood, DE	77
Petra Clark	Broxbourne, England	England	68
Marie Clay	Wellington, New Zealand	Auckland, NZ	81

	Born	**Died**	**Age**
Dave Cockrum	Pendleton, OR	Belpon, SC	63
Jim Cohen	Brisbane, Australia	England	58
Paul Cohen	Long Branch, NJ	Stanford, CA	72
Jack Cole	Lincoln, NE	Spearfish, SD	87
Harvey Colten	Houston, TX	New York City	68
Betty Comden	New York City	New York City	89
George Comstock	Niagra Falls, NY	Smithsburg, MD	92
Martin Conroy	New York City	Captiva, FL	84
Eva Crane	London	Slough, England	95
Jim Cronin	New York City	Dorset, England	55
G. Crowningshield	Colorado Springs, CO	Hightstown, NJ	87
June Csida	Los Angeles	Los Angeles	83
Angelo D'Agostino	Providence, RI	Nairobi, Kenya	80
Nelva de Falcone	Argentina	La Plata, Argentina	76
Robert DeForrest	Cleveland, OH	Washington, DC	72
Pierre de Gennes	Paris, France	Orsay, France	74
John Davis	Harpenden, England	Adjud, Romania	74
Alfred Desio	Geneva, NY	Los Angeles	74
Mary Douglas	San Remo, Italy	London	86
Anne Dowden	Denver, CO	Boulder, CO	99
George Duncan	Peterhead, England	England	64
Rogerio Duprat	Rio de Janeiro	Sao Paulo, Brazil	74
Alan Eames	Gardner, MA	Dummerston, VT	59
Don Edgren	Los Angeles	Eugene, OR	83
Walker Edmiston	St. Louis, MO	Woodland Hills, CA	81
Charles Ehret	New York City	Grayslake, IL	83
Sybil Elgar	London	England	92

	Born	**Died**	**Age**
Albert Ellis	Pittsburgh, PA	New York City	93
Ray Erlenborn	Denver, CO	West Hills, CA	92
Leonard Eron	Newark, NJ	Lindenhurst, IL	87
Ahmet Ertegun	Uskudar, Turkey	New York City	83
Joseph Eschbach	Detroit, MI	Bellevue, WA	74
Ray Evans	Salamanca, NY	Los Angeles	92
Nora Ezell	Brooksville, MS	Tuscaloosa, AL	88
Rhodes Fairbridge	Pinjarra, Australia	Amagansett, NY	92
David Fearn	England	England	68
Freddy Fender	San Benito, TX	Corpus Christi, TX	69
Eddie Feigner	Walla Walla, WA	Huntsville, AL	81
Celia Franca	London	Ottawa, Canada	85
Bill France, Jr.	Washington, DC	Daytona Beach, FL	74
Leonard Freed	New York City	New York State	77
Colin Fletcher	Cardiff, England	Monterey, CA	85
Kenneth Franklin	Alameda, CA	Boulder, CO	84
Helen Freeman	Everett, WA	Bellevue, WA	75
Sheldon Friedlander	New York City	Pacific Palisades, CA	79
Albert Friedman	Kansas City, MO	Los Angeles	86
Milton Friedman	New York City	San Francisco	94
Harold Froehlich	Minneapolis, MN	Maplewood, MN	84
Irene Galitzine	Tiflis, Russia	Rome, Italy	90
Norman Gaylord	New York City	Boynton Beach, FL	84
Clifford Geertz	San Francisco	Philadelphia	80
Magda Gerber	Budapest, Hungary	Silver Lake, CA	90
Ruth Gilbert	Philadelphia, PA	Monterey, CA	97
Donald Ginsberg	Chicago	Urbana, IL	73

	Born	**Died**	**Age**
Barbara Gittings	Vienna, Austria	Kennett Square, PA	74
John Gofman	Cleveland, OH	San Francisco	88
Richard Goodwin	Brookline, MA	East Lyme, CT	96
Leonard Greene	New York City	Mamaroneck, NY	88
Colin Greenwood	Glossop, England	England	72
Kenneth Greisen	Perth Amboy, NJ	Ithaca, NY	89
Boris Grushin	Moscow	Moscow	78
Paul Halmos	Budapest, Hungary	San Jose, CA	90
Larry Hamlin	Reidsville, NC	Pfafftown, NC	58
Jay Harnick	Chicago	New York City	78
Jay Haley	Midwest, WY	San Diego	83
Peter Hamill	Baltimore, MD	Annapolis, MD	80
Kelsie Harder	Perry County, TN	Potsdam, NY	84
Elizabeth Hay	St. Augustine, FL	Wayland, MA	80
Clarice Hayman	Los Angeles	Glasgow, MO	95
Chris Hayward	Bayonne, NJ	Beverly Hills, CA	81
Gloria Helfgott	New York City	Pacific Palisades, CA	79
Don Herbert	Waconia, MN	Los Angeles	89
Wally Herbert	York, England	Inverness, Scotland	72
Perry Henzell	Annotto Bay, Jamaica	Jamaica	70
Karen Hess	Blair, NE	New York City	88
John Heyning	San Jose, CA	Torrance, CA	50
Polly Hill	Ardmore, PA	Hockessin, DE	100
James Hillier	Brantford, Canada	Princeton, NJ	91
John Hogness	Oakland, CA	Seattle, WA	85
Arthur Holleb	New York City	Stamford, CT	85
Ida Hoos	Skowhegan, ME	Brookline, MA	94

	Born	Died	Age
Effie Mae Howard	Arkansas	Richmond, CA	70
Clark Howell	Kansas City, MO	Berkeley, CA	81
Pontus Hulten	Stockholm, Sweden	Stockholm, Sweden	82
Lamar Hunt	El Dorado, AR	Dallas	74
Joe Hunter	Jackson, TN	Detroit	79
Yale Joel	New York City	New York City	87
Michael Jackson	Yorkshire, England	London	65
Tommy Johnson	Los Angeles	Los Angeles	71
Russell Johnson	Berwick, PA	New York City	83
Arthur Jones	Arkansas	Ocala, FL	80
Winthrop Jordan	Worcester, MA	Oxford, MS	75
Leo Kanowitz	New York City	Berkeley, CA	81
Kawika Kapahulehua	Hilo, HI	Honolulu, HI	76
Mary Kaye	Detroit	Las Vegas	83
Jay Kennedy	Toledo, OH	Costa Rica	50
Ken Kennedy	Houston, TX	Houston, TX	61
Ralph Kent	Buffalo, NY	Kissimmee, FL	68
Alexander King	Glasgow, Scotland	England	98
Irene Kirkaldy	Baltimore, MD	Hayes, VA	90
George Kovacs	Vienna, Austria	New York City	80
Hilly Kristal	Hightstown, NJ	New York City	75
Russell Kruse	Auburn, IN	Ft. Wayne, IN	85
David Kritchevsky	Kharkov, Ukraine	Bryn Mawr, PA	86
Martin Kruskal	New York City	Princeton, NJ	81
Madeleine L'Engle	New York City	Litchfield, CT	88
Bernard Landau	Newark NJ	Cleveland, OH	80
Max Lanier	Denton, NC	Dunellon, FL	91

	Born	**Died**	**Age**
Paul Lauterbur	Sidney, OH	Urbana, IL	77
Percival Leach	Boonton, NJ	Hackettstown, NJ	80
Esther Lederberg	New York City	Stanford, CA	83
Nelson Leonard	Newark, NJ	Pasadena, CA	90
Aaron Lerner	Minneapolis	New Haven, CT	86
Henry LeTang	New York City	Las Vegas	91
John Lever	England	London	63
Lawrence Levine	New York City	Berkeley, CA	73
Carlos Lezama	New York City	New York City	83
Benjamin Libet	Chicago, IL	Davis, CA	91
Harold Lief	New York City	Bryn Mawr, PA	89
Sally Lilienthal	Portland, OR	San Francisco	87
Seymour Lipset	New York City	Arlington, VA	84
Jon Lucien	British Virgin Islands	Orlando, FL	65
Robert McFerrin Sr.	Marianna, AR	St. Louis, MO	85
Ian McGregor	Cambuslang, Great Britain	Great Britain	84
Enolia McMillan	Willow Grove, PA	Stevenson, MD	102
Jay McShann	Muskogee, OK	Kansas City, MO	90
Alan MacDiarmid	Masterton, New Zeland	Drexel Hill, PA	79
James MacKeith	Leamington Spa, England	London	68
Paul MacReady	New Haven, CT	Pasadena, CA	81
Gordon Macklin	Cleveland, OH	Delray Beach, FL	78
Theodore Maiman	Los Angeles	Vancouver	79
Michael Malone	San Rafael, CA	Chicago	64
Martin Manulis	New York City	Los Angeles	92
Janis Martin	Sutherlin, VA	Durham, NC	67
Will Maslow	Kiev, Ukraine	New York City	99

	Born	*Died*	*Age*
Rose Mattus	Poland	Westwood, NJ	90
Benjamin Meed	Warsaw, Poland	New York City	88
Florence Melton	Philadelphia, PA	Boca Raton, FL	95
Stanley Meltzoff	New York City	Red Bank, NJ	89
Gian Carlo Menotti	Cadegliano, Italy	Monaco	95
Ryszard Michalski	Kalusz, Poland	Fairfax, VA	70
Donald Michie	Rangoon, Burma	London, England	83
Tod Mikuriya	Bucks County, PA	Berkeley, CA	73
Stanley Miller	Oakland, CA	National City, CA	77
Hugo Moser	Bern, Switzerland	Baltimore, MD	82
Campbell Moses	Pittsburgh, PA	Saddle River, NJ	89
Evelyn Munro	New Orleans	Laguna Beach, CA	92
John Murra	Odessa, Ukraine	Ithaca, NY	90
Richard Mulvaney	Casper, WY	Fairfax, VA	88
Richard Musgrave	Konigstein, Germany	Santa Cruz, CA	84
Jack Myers	Boyds Mills, PA	Austin, TX	93
Ransom Myers	Lula, MS	Halifax, Nova Scotia	54
Ivan Nagy	Budapest, Hungary	Glenside, PA	86
Otto Natzler	Vienna, Austria	Los Angeles	99
Fernand Nault	Montreal	Montreal	85
Eric Newby	London	Surrey, England	86
Roy Newell	New York City	New York City	92
Martin Nodell	Philadelphia, PA	Muskego, WI	91
Parry O'Brien	Santa Monica, CA	Santa Clarita, CA	75
Anita O'Day	Chicago	Los Angeles	87
Anthony Oakhill	Leicester, England	Bristol, England	56
Jack Odell	London, England	London, England	87

	Born	Died	Age
Al Oerter	New York City	Fort Meyers, FL	71
Jules Olitski	Ukraine	New York City	84
Maureen Orcutt	New York City	Durham, NC	99
Stephen Osadebe	Nigeria	Nigeria	71
Donald Osterbrock	Cincinnati, OH	Santa Cruz, CA	82
Bodhan Paczynski	Vilnius, Lithuania	Princeton, NJ	67
Ralph Paffenbarger	Columbus, OH	Santa Fe, NM	84
Grace Paley	New York City	New York City	84
Dan Saxon Palmer	Budapest, Hungary	Santa Monica, CA	86
Wolfgang Panofsky	Berlin	Los Altos, CA	88
Wally Parks	Goltry, OK	Burbank, CA	94
Alfred Peet	Alkmaar, The Netherlands	Ashland, OR	87
David Perkins	Watertown, NY	Stanford, CA	87
Dorothy Perkins	Philadelphia, PA	Menlo Park, CA	84
William Peters	San Francisco	Guilford, CT	85
Abbe Pierre	Lyon, France	Paris	94
Nelson Polsby	Norwich, CT	Berkeley, CA	72
Jon Pritchard	Manchester, England	United Kingdom	64
Ferenc Puskas	Budapest, Hungary	Budapest, Hungary	79
Daniel Raichel	Paterson, NJ	El Cajon, CA	71
Bruce Rappaport	New Jersey	Walnut Creek, CA	64
Charles Remington	Reedville, VA	Hamden, CT	85
Ham Richardson	Baton Rouge, LA	New York City	73
George Rieveschl	Lockland, OH	Cincinnati, OH	91
Bernard Rimland	Cleveland, OH	El Cajon, CA	78
Max Roach	Newland, NC	New York City	83
Peter Roberts	Rugeley, England	England	82

	Born	Died	Age
Eddie Robinson	Jackson, LA	Ruston, LA	88
Julio Ruelas	Guadalajara, Mexico	Los Angeles	92
Anna Russell	Ontario, Canada	Australia	94
Mendy Samstein	New York City	New Lisbon, NY	68
Vincent Sardi, Jr.	New York City	Berlin, VT	91
Timo Sarpaneva	Helsinki, Finland	Helsinki, Finland	79
Gene Savoy	Bellingham, WA	Reno, NV	80
Mary Scheier	Salem, VA	Green Valley, AZ	99
Wally Schirra	Hackensack, NJ	San Diego	84
Jerry Schneider	Chicago, IL	Longboat Key, FL	87
Michael Seaton	Bristol, England	England	84
Atle Selberg	Langesund, Norway	Princeton, NJ	90
Ousmane Sembene	Casamance, Senegal	Dakar, Senegal	84
Jim Shoulders	Tulsa, OK	Henryetta, OK	79
Alan Shugart	Chino, CA	Monterey, CA	76
John Sieburth	Calgary, Canada	West Kingston, RI	79
Kai Siegbahn	Lund, Sweden	Angelholm Sweden	89
Spoony Singh	Jalandhar, India	Malibu, CA	83
Todd Skinner	Pinedale, WY	Yosemite, CA	47
Gerhard Skrobek	Leobschutz, Germany	Coburg, Germany	85
John Smith	London	England	83
Frank Snowden	York County, VA	Washington, DC	95
Edmund Sonnenblick	New Haven, CT	Darien, CT	74
Frank Speed	Weybridge, England	Nigeria	87
Andrew Spielman	New York City	Boston, MA	76
Fred Spira	Vienna, Austria	New York City	83
Frank Stanton	Muskegon, MI	Boston	98

	Born	**Died**	**Age**
Homer Stewart	Elba, MI	Altadena, CA	91
Larry Stewart	Bruce, MI	Kansas City, MO	58
V. Syromyatnikov	Russia	Moscow	73
Iwao Takamoto	Los Angeles	Los Angeles	81
Lenore Tawney	Lorain, OH	New York City	100
Glen Tetley	Cleveland, OH	West Palm Beach, FL	80
Leon Thal	New York City	Borrego Springs, CA	62
George Thomas	Boise, ID	State College, PA	92
Charles Tisdale	Athens, AL	Jackson, MS	80
John Todd	Ireland	Pasadena, CA	96
Mose Tolliver	Alabama	Montgomery, AL	86
Marc Torsilieri	Morristown, NJ	Somerville, NJ	48
George Trow	Greenwich, CT	Naples, Italy	63
Martin Trow	New York City	Kensington, CA	80
Walter Turnbull	Greenville, MS	New York City	62
Marguerite Vogt	Berlin, Germany	San Diego, CA	94
Tom Wagoner	Paris, KY	Longview, TX	75
Bradford Washburn	Cambridge, MA	Lexington, MA	96
Paul Watzlawick	Villach, Austria	Palo Alto, CA	85
Eugen Weber	Bucharest, Romania	Los Angeles	82
Martin Weber	New York City	New York City	102
Marvin Weinstein	Chicago, IL	Los Angeles	77
Milton Wexler	San Francisco	Santa Monica, CA	98
Gilbert White	Chicago, IL	Boulder, CO	94
Willye White	Money, MS	Chicago	67
Bill Whitman	Chicago	Bal Harbour, FL	92
Emmett Williams	Greenville, NC	Berlin, Germany	81

	Born	Died	Age
Jack Williamson	Bisbee, AZ	Portales, NM	98
H. Donald Wilson	New Rochelle, NY	Mitchellville, MD	82
Helmut Wimmer	Munich, Germany	Stuart, FL	80
Erich Windisch	Shoeneck, Germany	Vail, CO	89
Robert Wissler	Richmond, IN	Chicago	89
Lyman Wynne	Tyler, MN	Bethesda, MD	83
Marian Yarrow	Horicon, WI	Bethesda, MD	89
Ed Yost	Bristow, IA	Vadito, NM	87
Joseph Zuska	Chicago	Los Alamitos, CA	93

Sources

I relied on The New York Times, Los Angeles Times, The Washington Post, The Guardian and The Daily Telegraph, both of London, as my primary resources. These newspapers formed the basis of my research and I have drawn extensively from them. I used the Internet newspaper edition of the below sources as well as websites that offered additional material.

Newspaper Abbreviations:

NYT: The New York Times
LAT: Los Angles Times
G: The Guardian
T: The Daily Telegraph
WP: The Washington Post
AP: Associated Press

Robert Adler: NYT (Hafner), AP
Antonio Aguilar: LAT (Gurza), NYT (McKinley)
Ralph Alpher: LAT (Maugh), NYT (Wilford)
Robert Altman: LAT (McLellan), NYT (Lyman)
Momofuku Ando: LAT (Wallace), NYT (Hevesi)
Michelangelo Antonioni: NYT (Lyman), LAT (McLellan)
Bois Sec Ardoin: NYT (Pareles), G (Russell)
Paul Arizin: NYT (Goldstein), LAT
Rudolph Arnheim: WP (Bernstein), NYT (Fox)
Edmund Arnold: WP (Bernstein), NYT (Heller)
Robert Austrian: WP (Holley), NYT (Altman)
John Backus: LAT (Quinn), NYT (Lohr)

Roger Bacon: NYT (Pearce)

Albert Baez: LAT (Nelson)

Laurie Baker: NYT (Pandya)

Joseph Barbera: LAT (Solomon), NYT (Itzkoff), G (Gifford)

Jean Baudrillard: NYT (Cohen), LAT (Woo), G (Poole)

Henry Beachell: NYT (Pearce), Washington University Record (Purdy)

Eugene Bell: NYT (Pearce), I (Richmond)

Cuesta Benberry: NYT (Hevesi), WP (Sullivan)

Leonard Berg: NYT (Pearce)

Ingmar Bergman: NYT (Rothstein), LAT (Oliver)

Ruth Bernhard: LAT (Rourke), NYT (Gefter)

Jesus Blancornelas: NYT (McKinley), LAT (Tobar)

Paul Bohannan: LAT (Maugh)

Jane Bolin: NYT (Martin)

John Billings: NYT (Fox)

Edward Boyd: LAT (Stewart)

Edward Boyse: I (Richmond)

Ronald Bracewell: LAT (Maugh), NYT (Pearce)

Braguinha: NYT (Romero), brazill.com (Dalevi)

Edward Brandt: NYT (Altman), Maugh (LAT)

Desmond Briscoe: Answers.com, G (Niebur)

Todd Bright: NYT (Fox)

Joel Brodsky: WP (Schudel)

Ruth Brown: LAT (Powers/Lewis), WP (Bernstein)

Theodore Brunner: LAT (Noland)

Robert Buck: NYT (Fox)

Neville Butler: G (Goldstein), I

Job Bwayo: G (Moszynski)

Maureen Cannon: NYT (Fox)

George Cardinet, Jr.: LAT (Nelson)

Bob Carroll, Jr.: LAT (McLellan)

Anne Rogers Clark: NYT (Lavietes), AP

Dwight Chamberlain: NYT (Pearce)

Alfred Chandler: NYT (Martin)

Stella Chess: NYT (Pearce), NY Sun (Miller)
Petra Clark: G (Carroll)
Marie Clay: LAT (Woo), NYT (Fox)
Dave Cockrum: NYT (Martin), T
Jim Cohen: T
Paul Cohen: NYT (Pearce)
Jack Cole: LAT (Nelson), NYT (Fox)
Harvey Colten: NYT (Pearce)
Betty Comden: NYT (Berkvist), LAT (Rourke)
George Comstock: NYT (Altman), LAT (Maugh)
Martin Conroy: NYT (Fox)
Eva Crane: London Times, NYT (Martin), LAT (Nelson)
Jim Cronin: NYT (Hevesi), G (Bristow), I (Marren)
G. Robert Crowningshield: NYT (Pearce), gia.edu
June Bundy Csida: LAT (Stewart)
Angelo D'Agostino: WP (Holley), LAT (Rourke)
Nelva Mendez de Falcone: AP
Robert DeForrest: WP (Lamb)
Pierre-Gilles de Gennes: LT (Chang)
John Newsom-Davis: G (Weatherall), I (Vincent)
Alfred Desio: LAT (Segal)
Mary Douglas: NYT (Martin), London Times
Anne Dowden: LAT (Rourke)
George Duncan: G (Dawson/Wormstone)
Rogerio Duprat: NYT (Ratliff)
Alan Eames: NYT (Martin)
Don Edgren: LAT (Nelson), Orland Sentinel (Powers)
Walker Edmiston: AP, Variety
Charles Ehret: WP (Sullivan), Chicago Tribune
Sybil Elgar: National Autistic Society, G (Wing)
Albert Ellis: NYT (Kaufman), Woo (LAT)
Ray Erlenborn: LAT (McLellan)
Leonard Eron: NYT (Pearce), LAT (Stewart)
Joseph Eschbach: NYT (Pearce)

Ahmet Ertegun: NYT (Weiner), LAT (Boucher/Lewis), G (Sweeting), T
Ray Evans: LAT (McLellan)
Nora Ezell: NYT (Hevesi), LAT (Stewart)
Rhodes Fairbridge: NYT (Pearce)
David Fearn: G (Tilly), T
Eddie Feigner: NYT (Martin), AP
Freddy Fener: LAT (Nelson), AP, T
Colin Fletcher: LAT (Nelson), NYT (Hevesi)
Celia Franca: NYT (Anderson), G (Doob), LAT (Rourke)
Bill France, Jr.: NYT (Litsky), Hinton (LAT)
Kenneth Franklin: NYT (Martin)
Leonard Freed: G (Hopkinson), T, Photo District News (Lang)
Helen Freeman: Seattle Post-Intelligencer (McNerthney), NYT (Peterson)
Sheldon Friedlander: LAT (Nelson)
Albert Friedman: NYT (Fox), LAT (Woo)
Milton Friedman: NYT (Noble), LAT (Peterson)
Harold Froehlich: WP (Bernstein)
Irene Galitzine: NYT (Wilson)
Norman Gaylord: Newark Star-Ledger (Berkin), NYT (Pearce)
Clifford Geertz: NYT (Yarrow), G (Kuper), WP (Schudel)
Magda Gerber: LAT (Woo)
Ruth Gilbert: LAT (Thurber)
Donald Ginsberg: NYT (Pearce)
Barbara Gittings: NYT (Fox), pridesource.com
John Gofman: San Francisco Chronicle (Cote), LAT (Maugh)
Richard Goodwin: NYT (Hevesi), LAT (Nelson)
Leonard Greene: NYT (Bailey)
Colin Greenwood: G (Dawson/Thomson)
Kenneth Greison: NYT (Pearce)
Boris Grushin: NYT (Goldstein)
Jay Haley: NYT (Pearce), WP (Holley), LAT (Nelson)
Paul Halmos: NYT (Pearce)
Peter VanVechten Hamill: Baltimore Sun
Larry Hamlin: NYT (Robertson), LAT (Stewart)

Irene Morgan Kirkaldy: NYT (Goldstein), LAT (Woo)
George Kovacs: NYT (Hevesi)
Hilly Kristal: NYT (Sisario), London Times
David Kritchevsky: Philadelphia Daily News, NYT (Pearce)
Russell Kruse: NYT (Martin)
Martin Kruskal: NYT (Pearce), LAT (Maugh)
Madeleine L'Engle: NYT (Martin), LAT (Woo)
Bernard Landau: NYT (Pearce)
Max Lanier: NYT (Goldstein)
Paul Lauterbur: NYT (Chang), LAT (Maugh)
Percival Leach: NYT (Hevesi)
Esther Lederberg: LAT (Maugh), NYT (Pearce)
Nelson Leonard: LAT (Maugh), The Independent
Aaron Lerner: NYT (Pearce), Minneapolis Star Tribune (Cohen)
Henry LeTang: NYT (Fox)G (Monaghan)
John Lever: G (Caro/Kitney)
Lawrence Levine: LAT (Woo), NYT (Martin)
Carlos Lezama: NYT (Hevesi)
Benjamin Libet: San Francisco Chronicle (Perlman), LAT (Maugh)
Harold Lief: NYT (Pearce)
Sally Lilienthal: LAT (Nelson), WP (Sullivan)
Seymour Lispet: WP (Sullivan)
Jon Lucien: LAT (Thurber), NYT (Sisario)
Robert McFerrin Sr.: WP (Bernstein), AP
Ian McGregor: G (Prentice)
Enolia McMillan: Baltimore Sun (Brewington/Fuller)
Jay McShann: NYT (Keepnews), T, AP
Alan MacDiarmid: NYT (Chang), G (McLeish)
James MacKeith: T, I
Paul MacReady: LAT (Malnic), NYT (Martin)
Gordon Macklin: LAT (Pham), NYT (Meier)
Theodore Maiman: LAT (Johnson), NYT (Martin)
Michael Malone: NYT (Hevesi)
Martin Manulis: LAT (Noland), NYT (Martin)

Janis Martin: WP (Schudel), G (Laing)
Will Maslow: NYT (Hevesi)
Rose Mattus: NYT (Hevesi), T, AP, Manchester Evening News (Ramsey)
Benjamin Meed: NYT (Fox)
Florence Melton: NYT (Hevesi), LAT (Rourke)
Stanley Meltzoff: NYT (Hevesi)
Gian Carol Menotti: NYT (Holland), LAT (Oliver), G (Lane)
Ryszard Michalski: WP (Schudel)
Donald Michie: London Times, NYT (Pearce), G (Muggleton)
Tod Mikuriya: NYT (Fox)
Stanley Miller: LAT (Maugh), NYT (Wade)
Hugo Moser: LAT (Maugh), WP (Vedantam)
Campbell Moses, Jr.: NYT (Pearce)
Richard Mulvaney: WP (Sullivan)
Evelyn Munro: LAT (Woo)
John Murra: NYT (Hevesi), G (Harris)
Richard Musgrave: NYT (Walsh)
Jack Myers: NYT (Hevesi), Palm Beach Post (Vail)
Ransom Myers: NYT (Dean), LAT (Weiss)
Ivan Nagy: NYT (Carey)
Otto Natzler: LAT (Luther)
Fernand Nault: NYT (Kisselgoff), cbc.ca
Eric Newby: NYT (Fox), G (George), T
Roy Newell: NYT (Genocchio)
Martin Nodell: Newsday, AP
Parry O'Brien: NYT (Litsky), espn.com
Anita O'Day: NYT (Chinen), LAT (McLellan), G (Fordham), T
Anthony Oakhill: T
Jack Odell: NYT (Martin), I (Chapman)
Al Oerter: NYT (Litsky), AP
Jules Olitski: NYT (Genocchio)
Maureen Orcutt: WP (Sullivan), NYT (Litsky)
Chief Stephen Osita Osadebe: LAT (Stewart)
Donald Osterbrock: LAT (Johnson), NYT (Pearce)

Bohdan Paczynski: NYT (Pearce), LAT (Maugh)
Ralph Paffenbarger: NYT (Pearce), LAT (Nelson)
Grace Paley: NYT (Fox), LAT (Woo)
Dean Saxon Palmer: LAT (Noland)
Wolfgang Panofsky: San Francisco Chronicle (Perlman)
San Jose Mercury News (May), NYT (Pearce)
Wally Parks: LAT (Glick)
Alfred Peet: San Francisco Chronicle (Raine), NYT (Marshall)
David Perkins: San Francisco Chronicle (Allday), LAT (Maugh)
Dorothy Perkins: San Francisco Chronicle (Allday), LAT (Maugh)
William Peters: NYT (Fox), LAT (Stewart)
Abbe Pierre: NYT (Martin), AP
Nelson Polsby: NYT (Martin), LAT (Woo), G (Hodgson)
Jon Pritchard: G (Simons)
Ferenc Puskas: LAT (Jones)
Daniel Raichel: NYT (Pearce)
Bruce Rappaport: LAT (Nelson)
Charles Lee Remington: AP, NYT (Yoon), LAT (Maugh)
Ham Richardson: NYT (Goldstein), Tennis Week
George Rieveschl: Cincinnati Enquirer (O'Farrell), NYT (Hevesi)
Bernard Rimland: NYT (Carey), LAT (Maugh)
Max Roach: NYT (Keepnews), LAT (Heckman)
Peter Roberts: T, animalliberationfront.com
Eddie Robinson: NYT (Wallace/Litsky), LAT (Dufresne)
Julio Ochoa Ruelas: LAT (Stewart)
Anna Russell: NYT (Rothstein), T
Mendy Samstein: NYT (Martin)
Vincent Sardi, Jr.: NYT (Grimes)
Timo Sarpaneva: NYT (Martin)
Gene Savoy: NYT (Martin), AP (Griffith)
Mary Scheier: NYT (Heydarpour)
Wally Schirra: LAT (Malnic), NYT (Goldstein)
Jerry Schneider: NYT
Michael Seaton: G (Zeippen)

Atle Selberg: NYT (Pearce), LAT (Maugh)
Ousmane Sembene: NYT (Scott), LAT (McLellan)
Jim Shoulders: Dallas Morning News (Knocke), NYT (Goldstein)
Alan Shugart: NYT (Markoff)
John Sieburth: NYT (Martin)
Kai Siegbahn: NYT (Pearce), LAT (Maugh)
Spoony Singh: LAT (Nelson), NYT (Martin)
Todd Skinner: NYT (Stallman)
Gerhard Skrobek: NYT (Fox)
John Smith: G (Drury)
Frank Snowden: NYT (Fox), WP (Bernstein)
Edmund Sonnenblick: NYT (Altman)
Frank Speed: G (Barber/Simmonds)
Andrew Spielman: NYT (Pearce), Boston Globe (Marquard)
Fred Spira: NYT (Hevesi)
Frank Stanton: NYT (Noble), LAT (Luther)
Homer Stewart: LAT (Maugh), NYT (Pearce)
Larry Stewart: Kansas City Star (Franey), AP
Vladimir Syromyatnikov: LAT
Iwao Takamoto: AP
Lenore Tawney: NYT (Cotter)
Glen Tetley: NYT (Kisselgoff), G (Parry)
Leon Thal: NYT (Pearce), LAT (Woo)
George Thomas: NYT (Pearce)
Charles Tisdale: LAT (Stewart)
John Todd: LAT (Maugh), caltech.edu
Marc Torsilieri: NYT (Martin)
George Trow: NYT (Fox), NY Sun (Bernhard)
Martin Trow: NYT (Martin), UC Berkeley News
Walter Turnbull: NYT (Sisario), LAT
Marguerite Vogt: NYT (Pearce). London Times
Tom Wagoner: AP, LAT
Bradford Washburn: Boston Globe (Bailey/Ryan), NYT (Pearce)
Paul Watzlawick: NYT (Pearce)

Eugen Weber: NYT (Yarrow)
Martin Weber: NYT (Heller)
Hans Wegner: NYT (Colman), Architectural Record
Marvin Weinstein: LAT (Nelson)
Milton Wexler: NYT (Martin), LAT (Woo)
Gilbert White: WP (Sullivan)
Willye White: NYT (Litsky)
Bill Whitman: NYT (Karp)
Emmett Williams: NYT (Heydarpour)
Jack Williamson: LAT (McLellan), NYT (Fox), T
H. Donald Wilson: WP (Sullivan)
Helmut Wimmer: NYT (Hevesi)
Erich Windisch: NY (Hevesi)
Robert Wissler: NYT (Pearce), uchospitals.edu
Lyman Wynne: NYT (Carey), stronghealth.com
Marian Radke-Yarrow: NYT (Hevesi), WP (Weil)
Ed Yost: NYT (Hevesi)
Joseph Zuska: LAT (Stewart)

978-0-595-48945-9
0-595-48945-1

www.ingramcontent.com/pod-product-compliance
Lightning Source LLC
Chambersburg PA
CBHW020436290526
45785CB00002B/883